Declaration of (Dis) Interest

musings on modern music
from an old punk rocker

Bart A. Lazar

Cover design: Onur Burc
Back cover summary: Kenneth J. Helin

Published by Teacup Ventures LLC, Chicago, IL

ISBN: 9798718568356

Forward

By: Don Hedeker, The Polkaholics
https://polkaholics.wixsite.com/polkaholics

Bart Lazar's DJ emails: notes from the underground frontline

If there is anyone who knows more about underground and independent rock music in the world than Bart Lazar, I have yet to hear of them. Bart's annual postings from SXSW have always been something to look forward to and savor every syllable as he expertly described the wide collection of bands from all over the world that would convene in Austin every March. These are included in this collection, which also includes his many DJ emails to announce his gigs at Sportsman's Club and other venues in Chicago. What makes this collection so special is the utter enthusiasm that Bart projects about the music he loves and wants to turn us onto. It reminds you of the first time you heard a great band in grammar school, high school, or college and JUST HAD to tell everyone about them. And although Bart is a walking encyclopedia of music, he never lets the details get in the way of a good story – it's always about the energy and spirit of the music, and never who played on what for what reason and under what circumstances. Bart knows all of this for sure, but these emails remind one of the reason we all love music in the first place – it's the singer, not the song! Well, actually, it is the song, but it's certainly not the Under Assistant West Coast Promo Man! Sorry, couldn't resist the early Stones references ☺ So dive deep into this collection and you will be mesmerized by Bart's astute assessments of all things cool and hip in music, but without all the baggage that cool and hip usually bring with. Like the music he champions, Bart is the real deal and his writings are like a three-chord anthem to fun, Fun, FUN!!!

Contents

Chapter 1: Me-Shuga--I Can Imagine Myself at a Crazy/Special Sportsman's DJ Night--Saturday February 27

Subject: Me-Shuga--I Can Imagine Myself at a Crazy/Special Sportsman's DJ Night--Saturday February 27

From: Lazar, Bart
Sent: Monday, February 22, 2016 8:53 PM

Hey, we have almost made it through winter Chicago and after a month of Super Bowl and other current commercials featuring music from The Julie Ruin, Pylon, The Ramones, Bowie and Tom Tom Club and Pylon it time to re-make/re-model and unearth some cultural icons from our past, present and future.

For your imminent consideration, I am excited to have a special guest DJ to present and share with you, Adam Rosen the owner of Shuga records, who will help me purvey my monthly that harmonious cacophony at the friendly Sportsman's Club, 948 N. Western, this Saturday February 27 from 10-245.

So come out, grab a beer, amaro or one of the awesome daily cocktails---maybe it will be warm enough for some patio time and hear some spontaneity.

Chapter 2: 2016 SXSW Report---Sportsman's March 26

Subject: 2016 SXSW Report---Sportsman's March 26

From: Lazar, Bart
Sent: Tue, Mar 22, 2016, 11:08 PM

Happy Spring Everyone. Well, I just got back from Austin an sitting in my safe Chicagoan home, so I wanna share some of my 2016 observations again.

For those in Chicago, I will be playing vinyl from many of the bands mentioned at Sportsman's Club on Saturday March 26 from around 10:00 on.

EVERYTHING HAPPENS FOR A REASON, OR NOT AT ALL

There is a reason why events unnerve anyone. At SXSW everyone can find a different story. And that story plays out differently with every choice you make. Imagine: when you choose to eat at one restaurant you are turning down hundreds, if not thousands of deserving establishments in your fair city---at SX when you affirmatively head down one of many diverging roads to see a band, you are implicitly (but not knowingly) rejecting at least hundreds of other potentially deserving bands--each of whom you can hear groan when they learn they were not let in your tourney--at least on that day or that evening. Simultaneously, you have created a path where anything could still happen--just be ready.

I am not a fatalist, I believe in luck and that an individual's actions can increase the likelihood luck will migrate towards you. Yet neither you nor an event's organizers can account for something as unnerving as a tornado/severe thunderstorm such that even a behemoth like SX can be forced to head for cover. On Friday night, this happened, forcing the closing of many outdoor venues and cancellation of many shows, including probably one I thought I was headed for. Instead of cashing in and choosing NCAA > SX or some other show I grabbed an umbrella and stormed towards the alley entrance to Barracuda outdoor to find the gate shut. So I decided to check out the Barracuda indoor entrance, even though it is usually a second and different venue at night, and was fortunate to learn the venue had pivoted by choosing to combine two showcases into one by moving the outdoor showcases indoors--taping off an area in the middle of the floor as the "outdoor" stage.

By converting floor space into a stage, the Barracuda "backyard" showcase suddenly was transformed, into the indie roots of SXSW, an intensely personal diy space with virtually no sound check, no monitors to speak of, an unmiked drum set and the band performing "in the trapezoid" face to face with themselves and/or the audience. For Providence punks GymShorts, this eliminated stage diving--the lead singer/guitarist simply sang directly at, and moshed with guitar and the crowd. Los Angeles' Death Valley Girls (after a team huddle) chose an alignment where the lead singer and guitarists played and sang directly across from, at and to the drummer--which created intimacy within the band as well as with those watching. It imbued a stormy, blah kind of night full of long into a reaffirmation of what SXSW is all about--raw, new music, connection with performers and just a tinge of nervousness about what might happen next.

And that made all the difference.

OK, so what about the bands?

Downtown Boys (Hole in the Wall) -- There is enough to write a whole separate article about Victoria Ruiz and her crew from Providence (how did that get to be a punk epicenter?). They are a fiery combination of anti-racist and pro-people diatribes served with a side of thick sax/guitar pulse activating both the body and mind to betterment. The commentary/intros are as important, meaningful and entertaining as the songs, challenging what right the Texas lawmakers or US Supreme Court have to tell people what they can or can't do with their bodies, the importance of words and context, the meaning of Malcolm X, the evils of slumlords, and how Bruce Springsteen uses more punk words in his songs like "fire," "burn" and "desire" than most "punk" bands. In fact, even though many compare Downtown Boys to X Ray Spex because they are a punk band with a key saxophone player, Victoria pronounced that her band is closer to Bruce Springsteen and the E Street Band!

Party Static (Volstead Room) -- A chaotic, beautiful mess of a good time from Dallas, featuring two female vocalists who alternatively sing together and then AT each other with almost an accusatory nature reminiscent of Mika Miko. They dance and bump into each other while roaming freeform on top of a pulsing, driving backbeat and black and decker scuzzy guitars.

Fear of Men (Sidewinder)--The ethereal floating vocals of Jessica Weiss combine with the swirly guitar rhythms of Dan Falvey and intentionally off the beaten path drums to provide a haunting pop tableau. About to release their second album, this Brighton group is focusing more on creating space for vocals, eschewing hypnotic guitar interplay for dream time.

Thee Oh Sees (Hotel Vegas-Outside). Now in their 17th year at SX, John Dwyer and his psychotic garage rock express train about to go off the rails are one of my SX traditions of a decade or more!. Basically playing in residence each day, either heading the afternoon at 6 pm or the evening at 1 am, they even started their She Shreds' set early so they could play a longer set! After changing the band completely last year (not necessarily for the best) John has re-adopted a double drum line up which allows a stronger and faster backbeat for his frenzied revved up Nuggets-infused raves.

Haelos -- (Space 2420-what used to be the backyard of Urban Outfitters) --A chill, kind of trip hop band from London that provides a shimmering, moody sound track for what the start or more likely is the end of a late night clubbing session. Repetitive boy/girl vocals, electronica and percussion with some Edge guitar and interspersed recorded historical voices to make you sway--lull your head, shoulders, and ultimately your hips, into submission.

Cosmonauts -- (Hotel Vegas Bar) These slackers from Santa Cruz are kind of the west coast version of Parquet Courts, able to outstone the Rolling Stones (think of an amped up Gimme Shelter).

Future Punx (Sidecar)-- Talking Heads and Devo are mashed together and brought to a new generation by Brooklyn (you tell me if they are hip or geek) sters.

Charles Bradley & His Extraordinaires (Stubb's) --- His escape from the Brooklyn projects is tracked in a 2012 documentary and now at 67, this soul singer is starting to hit the height of his popularity, using a full horn section to help him channel the energy of James Brown and the uplifting spirit of Al Green. that can force you to shake your tail as he On "Changes" from his upcoming release, he slowly but forcefully preaches with bonechilling elegiac sadness about his mother's passing. He shows the breadth of human emotion with one voice and an earthy horn section.

Diet Cig (Hole in the Wall) --A two piece drum and guitar group form New Paltz, New York, combines adolescent Liz Phair themes with early Wavves emotional power punk, punctuated by Alex Luciano's whirling dervish kicks and leaps in between verses. Infectious.

Death Valley Girls -(Barricuda--on the floor)- Not letting the whole stage on the floor thing get them down, this LA band charged into their Cramp-infused insistent bloozy guitar grind and fluesy vocals including their song "No Reason" (from which I lifted the title of this piece).

Oscar (Space 2420)-- You wouldn't expect a tall Brit wearing a Disney-character jacket could deliver deep dark vocals and lush harmonies. But when this English popstar gets revved up his music gets , dare I say, Smiths-like.

The Foreign Resort (Tiniest Bar in Texas)--Post punk dark wave dance music lives on in this band from Copenhagen, Denmark. Propulsive early Cure lead bass guitars and automatic drums support roaring and chiming guitars and plaintive vocals about how "everybody is empty now" or how "you are my downfall." Depression can be so uplifting!

Iggy Pop's Post Pop Depression (ACL Moody Theatre). I admit to being a late adopter of Iggy, but he certainly is one of the Seven World Wonders at this point. A buzzsaw of energy, punching, kicking, preening, waving, daring the audience to come down an f__k him, stage diving--he is literally, figuratively and bodily busting at the seams to keep doing something. Maybe that is the point: like his mentor that he is gonna go out fighting on his own terms. But despite or maybe because of his electrifying persona, the sound of the new material from Josh Homme of Queens of the Stone Age did not quite do it for me--a bit too slick and not enough of the Iggy primal nature in the sound as in the performance and the feel.

People are always asking about how crowded SX has become after so many years and what impact that has. The impact is significant. Certain places, like Hotel Vegas, with, essentially 4 venues with 2 or 3 bands playing at once have now been "discovered" so that you need to get there early or wait in line or both. And, you have to make a more considered decision if you leave, because you might not get back in. Also, many day parties have become democratized, so that badges do not give you priority as often as they used to (another reason why badges are less relevant now). Sometimes that means trying new or retrying old venues. For example, when downtown and east side got too crowded, I headed for the drag--by the University of Texas, where many of the same groups were playing to much smaller crowds. I escaped there a few years ago and saw Wild Flag, Times New Viking and an early version of Cloud Nothings in one of the best curated showcases, so it was time for a return visit!

Chapter 3: All Messed Up and Ready to Go(*)--This Saturday 5/14 Sportsman's Club + Lizard Lounge Drinks

Subject: All Messed Up and Ready to Go(*)-- This Saturday 5/14 Sportsman's Club + Lizard Lounge Drinks

From: Lazar, Bart
Sent: Thu, May 12, 2016, 11:16 PM

While we wait for Summer to kick in in Chicago there's a lot to celebrate, commemorate and otherwise rate.

But beware the ides of ratings--they are not of your own experience and soul. I was reminded by the friend of a friend my own mantra of seeing/hearing for myself what a band was like, rather than accept another's experience. Don't leave it (music, food, wine, anything) completely to another's rating or recommendation--go out there and use your senses so you know how it feels yourself. Reification in point was a remarkable rebirth and commemoration from a band I expected to stick a fork in--Guns N' Roses (Yeah, I know, but I was there). Their commemorative rebirth of royalty ranged from the heartfelt opening chords of Johnny Thunders' You Can't Put Your Arms Around a Memory to Slash's Wish You Were Here to Axl Rose's heartfelt dedication of an entire set to Prince. All the while showing a visceral gut punching and kick assing vitality of a band with a lot to prove.

So this Saturday come hang out at Sportsman's Club as we conjure all vinyl harmony through 50 + years of rock and roll and a variety of communal experiences from British invasion to current indie with the usual heavy dose of punk to post punk wanna dance. In addition to celebrating birthdays of Joey Ramone, Eric Burdon, Sid Vicious and other friends, Graham, Laura and crew will be making drinks straight out of the Lizard Lounge drink menu (circa 1987), which thanks to Lauree and Chuck from Club Foot we are able to perpetuate.

As always there is more to be left unsaid, so make sure to let Sportsman's Club be all or part of your journey.

Saturday May 14, 2016 10:00 (or maybe a little bit before)-close.
948 N. Western Ave.

*The Records.
https://www.youtube.com/watch?v=hCKntsygVlA [updated link]

If you want another video, check out this great set by Thee Oh Sees in the back of Boticelli's, an Italian restaurant on South Congress in Austin in 2013. There were about 20 people there and I was right behind the person videotaping.
https://www.youtube.com/watch?v=lcXlAfPwbSE

Johnny Thunders=John Anthony Genzale, Jr.,
Slash=Saul Hudson
Eric Burdon=Eric Burdon
Axl Rose

Chapter 4: Memories: Like the Corner of Augusta and Western--DJ thing Saturday May 28 at Sportsmans

Subject: Memories: Like the Corner of Augusta and Western--DJ thing Saturday May 28 at Sportsmans

From: Lazar, Bart
Sent: Thu, May 26, 2016 at 10:32 PM

If only memories can be extracted from one's brain and dropped into a pensieve like in Harry Potter, or recorded on internal brainwave images and experientially replayed like in Til the End of the World or traded and injested like a drug in Strange Days.

I wish I remembered everything I discussed with Joey Ramone when I popped into Paul's Lounge at Third and Tenth to meet up to day drink, shoot some pool and watch some sports. Joey Ramone sat down at the bar next to us to order some drinks and what he called "pigeon sandwiches" basically a turkey club. Joey's loft was over in The St. Mark on East Ninth Street and he liked to hang out at Paul's (Joey named it along with venerable institutions like The Ritz, Cat Club, Pyramid, Limelight and Save the Robots in his "New York City").

Joey mentioned that he was hiding from his manager Monte because he had a gig in Allentown, Pennsylvania that night and he really did not want to get in the van to do the show. As you can learn from watching the sad Ramones Doc End of the Century or reading Marc Bell's autobiography, the Ramones would take a van to virtually any show within a 3-5 hour driving radius and come home THE SAME NIGHT to save money on hotels. During the trip the band and any girlfriends/wives sat in assigned seats and Johnny and Joey, in particular, would not talk to each other at all (stemming from the fact that Johnny took Joey's girlfriend).

After a few drinks Joey laid his head on the bar and took a nap. When he woke up, he was really excited about the basketball game--particularly those "Dukes" (the Duke basketball team) and ordered up a pigeon sandwich platter to share. Eventually Monte found him and cajoled/dragged him out of the bar.

So celebrate Joey and many others here and within our internal leaky caldrons by doing what you want to do --which will hopefully include hanging out this Saturday May 28 at Sportsman's Club 948 N. Western. 10 (or maybe a little earlier) to close. The patio will be open, some of the nicest and best bartenders in Chicago will be serving, drink from the amaro machine and listen to some vinyl. I'm driving the trolley and playing miscellaneous percussion.

Chapter 5: SCHEDULING CHANGE---EARLIER START- 6-10 PM. Memories: Like the Corner of Augusta and Western--DJ thing Saturday May 28 at Sportsmans

Subject: SCHEDULING CHANGE---EARLIER START- 6-10 PM. Memories: Like the Corner of Augusta and Western--DJ thing Saturday May 28 at Sportsmans

From: Lazar, Bart
Sent: Sat, May 28, 2016 at 11:46 AM

I apologize for the spam, but due to circumstances beyond my control, and since its Summer, I am going to do an early set tonight from 6-10 pm. This way all of you that complain I start too late can come out this afternoon/evening. Have a great weekend

If only memories can be extracted from one's brain and dropped into a pensieve like in Harry Potter, or recorded on internal brainwave images and experientially replayed like in Til the End of the World or traded and injested like a drug in Strange Days.

I wish I remembered everything I discussed with Joey Ramone when I popped into Paul's Lounge at Third and Tenth to meet up to day drink, shoot some pool and watch some sports. Joey

Ramone sat down at the bar next to us to order some drinks and what he called "pigeon sandwiches" basically a turkey club. Joey's loft was over in The St. Mark on East Ninth Street and he liked to hang out at Paul's (Joey named it along with venerable institutions like The Ritz, Cat Club, Pyramid, Limelight and Save the Robots in his "New York City").

Joey mentioned that he was hiding from his manager Monte because he had a gig in Allentown, Pennsylvania that night and he really did not want to get in the van to do the show. As you can learn from watching the sad Ramones Doc End of the Century or reading Marc Bell's autobiography, the Ramones would take a van to virtually any show within a 3-5 hour driving radius and come home THE SAME NIGHT to save money on hotels. During the trip the band and any girlfriends/wives sat in assigned seats and Johnny and Joey, in particular, would not talk to each other at all (stemming from the fact that Johnny took Joey's girlfriend).

After a few drinks Joey laid his head on the bar and took a nap. When he woke up, he was really excited about the basketball game--particularly those "Dukes" (the Duke basketball team) and ordered up a pigeon sandwich platter to share. Eventually Monte found him and cajoled/dragged him out of the bar.

So celebrate Joey and many others here and within our internal leaky caldrons by doing what you want to do --which will hopefully include hanging out this Saturday May 28 at Sportsman's Club 948 N. Western. 10 (or maybe a little earlier) to close. The patio will be open, some of the nicest and best bartenders in Chicago will be serving, drink from the amaro machine and listen to some vinyl. I'm driving the trolley and playing miscellaneous percussion.

Chapter 6: Chapter 6: NO LOLLA, POST LOLLA OR _____ LOLLA -- THERE WILL BE PLENTY OF INDIE, POST PUNK AND MORE SATURDAY AT SPORTSMAN'S CLUB

Subject: NO LOLLA, POST LOLLA OR LOLLA -- THERE WILL BE PLENTY OF INDIE, POST PUNK AND MORE SATURDAY AT SPORTSMAN'S CLUB

From: Lazar, Bart
Sent: Thu, Jul 28, 2016, 12:09 AM

Well it's the sort of 25th anniversary (with some gaps) of our good friend and turf destructor. So I thought a fun exercise would be to look at each year and pick one or more bands that have played Lolla each year that remain part of my vinyl repertoire today. There are a bunch more but this will have to do for now!

I will probably have all this in stock this Saturday plus my (un)usual assortment of Pre and Post Punk Progressive and Propulsive Pop and Wave, British Invasion, and maybe a little bit of stuff people have been dancing to for the last 39 years or so predominantly from bands that have not and will never play

Lolla. So whether you are stumbling in from before, during or aftershow or just looking for a cool place to grab a drink from some of the friendliest and most knowledgeable bartenders in the city (including ahem--the Time Out Chicago 2016 bartender of the year) and hang out you know where to go.

Saturday, July 30 from 10 pm to close at Sportsman's Club., 948 North Western Avenue.

1991--Siousxie and the Banshees
1992-Jesus and Mary Chain
1993-Royal Trux
1994--Tribe Called Quest/ L7/ Shonen Knife
1995-Patti Smith
1996-Ramones
1997- Devo
2003- The Donnas
2005--The Ponys
2006-Sleater-Kinney
2007- CSS/Yeah Yeah Yeahs/Stooges
2008- Yeasayer
2009-No Age/Santigold/Raveonettes
2010- Warpaint
2011- Best Coast
2012-Black Angels/Sabbath/Dum Dum Girls
2013-The Cure
2014-Parquet Courts
2015-War Against Drugs/Tame Impala
2016-Kurt Vile/LCD/Haelos

Chapter 7: One thing is certain (I think)--Sportsman's DJ Saturday October 29

Subject: One thing is certain (I think)--Sportsman's DJ Saturday October 29

From: Lazar, Bart
Sent: Thu, Oct 27, 2016, 11:44 PM

I'm uncertain about a lot of things, I could but can't blame it on

- the election;
- the World Series,
- Halloween; or
- the rotation of the Earth;

but important things are messing me up. Like deciding whether to watch/listen to the Cubs or Peter Hook tomorrow, and if I do can I listen to the announcers any more, or whether to have a Halloween costume or not and whether I can possibly pull off a costume other than a fake Joey Ramone (or Ozzy Osborne, John Lennon, Slash) and why Billy Bragg knows more about US politics than I do.

I can't resolve all those dilemma (or is it dilemmae?--like I said I am uncertain--just kidding auto-correct covered that one),

But I can guarantee that from 10 to about Gary U.S. Bonds time (that's 1/4 2 3) I will be purveying post-cubs, post-punk and a whole lot more

At Sportsman's Club
948 N. Western Ave
Saturday October 29.

And just in case you are interested, it is great watching the game in the backyard--I'm sure I'll be there and with the way they are using relievers, the game will go past 10.

And don't forget to vote (see attachment).

When one voice rules the nation
Just because they're on top of the pile
Doesn't mean their vision is the clearest
The voices of the people
Are falling on deaf ears
Our politicians all become careerists
They must declare their interests
But not their company cars
Is there more to a seat in parliament
Then sitting on your arse
And the best of all this bad bunch
Are shouting to be heard
Above the sound of ideologies clashing
Outside the patient millions
Who put them into power
Expect a little more back for their taxes
Like school books, beds in hospitals
And peace in our bloody time
All they get is old men grinding axes
Who've built their private fortunes
On the things they can rely
The courts, the secret handshake

The Stock Exchange and the old school tie
For God and Queen and Country
All things they justify
Above the sound of ideologies clashing
God bless the civil service
The nations saving grace
While we expect democracy
They're laughing in our face
And although our cries get louder
Their laughter gets louder still
Above the sound of ideologies clashing
Billy Bragg--just him and Woody Guthrie's legacy--Ideology.

Chapter 8: Reasons to be Thankful Part III --Everyday People (and Sportsman's DJ)

Subject: Reasons to be Thankful Part III --Everyday People (and Sportsman's DJ)

From: Lazar, Bart
Sent: Sun, Nov 20, 2016, 8:05 PM

I guess we now know that we are more caring, tolerant, kind, just, egalitarian, humanistic.. (I could go on and on) than our future fearful leader.

That may not be saying much, but……... We now need to be an anti-hate group--we hate hate..

So where does that leave us in this mosh pit of our country?

While bouncing and parrying to the beat of our lives, please keep your periscope up and watch out for each other. If someone has been knocked down----shield them when they are vulnerable. Offer a shoulder to help someone steady themselves as they re-put on their shoe (I suggest wearing zip up boots for the next 4 years) or help to look for something that is lost in the shuffle when you are able. If you have to step up to protect someone-be polite, firm and deflect tat person who is not engaged in Brownian motion but looking to cause pain. If you accidentally pogo on a toe--share an oral or visual "sorry about that chief" or if someone accidentally does it to you, an "ok".

Just remember that even in a mosh pit--if something is intentionally not respectful and/or harmful to others ---we ought not dance idly by.

This is our venue, and our mosh pit. Let's follow the golden rule.

But don't forget to dance and enjoy the show.

I interrupt this public service announcement to say that after you have had your fill of turkey or tofurkey, come on down to the friendly confines of The Sportsman's Club, 948 N. Western on Saturday November 26. Google says people typically spend 45 minutes to 2 hours there, but I will be there for 4+ hours--10:00-2:45 playing 50+ years of pre and post-punk progressive pop (and more) vinyl and helping to create community (or scaring people out) through music.

Chapter 9: Holiday in Cambodia (I mean Sportmans)--Chanukah/Xmas Saturday December 24

Subject: Holiday in Cambodia (I mean Sportmans)--Chanukah/Xmas Saturday December 24

From: Lazar, Bart
Sent: Thu, Dec 22, 2016, 3:01 PM

I don't own that many Xmas songs, so I may be in trouble around here--but I don't own too many (if any) Hanukkah or Chanukah songs on vinyl either.

That could be a good thing as I close out the year at Sportsman's Club on Saturday December 24, from 10-closing.

I wish you peace, love, friendship, health and harmony (unless of course you like cacophony) in 2017. -Bart

LifeWork in Progress-2017
This year was filled with tragedy,
sonically + visually,
political-LEE, controversially and personally
sometimes it's hard to handle, individually,
but remember, ultimately
everyday people can resolve things together, and differently,

we've better things to do, to be free
and the wine bottle is way more than half full in this tower of song.

Or as Johnny Mercer and Harold Arlen put it in 1944 --a year which had to be as challenging for the US and the world as today-
You've got to accentuate the positive
Eliminate the negative
Latch on to the affirmative
Don't mess with Mister In-Between
You've got to spread joy up to the maximum
Bring gloom down to the minimum
Have faith or pandemonium
Liable to walk upon the scene
My only comment is pandemonium in the right time and place, and with the right people ain't that bad-- if done right!

One right time and place would be Sportsman's Club- 948 N. Western, Saturday December 24. 10 onward and upward.

Here are my best ofs in progress 2017 (no apparent order or commentary yet)

Most Memorable Non-Festival Shows

PONY'S (Empty Bottle)
NEGATIVE SCANNER (as best as I can recall, Bric-a-Brac records, Empty Bottle, Café Rectum and Hideout)
BRUCE SPRINGSTEEN (Milwaukee).
THEE OH SEES (Thalia Hall, Empty Bottle).
PRINCE RAMA (Schuba's/SXSW)
NIGHT BEATS (Beat Kitchen)
COSMONAUTS (East Room).
CHARLES BRADLEY (Thalia Hall and Space)
MEKONS (Hideout)
TELEVISION (930 Club)
GLENN BRANCA (Roulette)
METRIC (House of Blues)

JULIE RUIN (Lincoln Hall)
PETER HOOK AND THE LIGHT (2xMetro)

Most Memorable Festival/Outdoor Shows (though I did not make it to Pitchfork this year)

DIET CIG (Milwaukee Ave Fest)
DOWNTOWN BOYS (SXSW)
FEAR OF MEN (SXSW/Schubas)
GUNS N' ROSES (Coachella)
JOY FORMIDABLE (Lolla)
SLEATER-KINNEY (Riotfest)
BLEACHED (SXSW/Riotfest)
SPECIALS (Riotfest/Concord)
LCD SOUNDSYSTEM (Coachella/Lolla)
HAELOS (SXSW/Lolla)
PARTY STATIC (SXSW)
KURT VILE (Lolla)

Chapter 10: Maybe We'll Make it After All--2nd Anniversary at Sportsman's --Tomorrow January 28

Subject: Maybe We'll Make it After All--2nd Anniversary at Sportsman's --Tomorrow January 28

From: Lazar, Bart
Sent: Fri, Jan 27, 2017, 5:23 PM

Just a quick break in the winter of our discontent to celebrate my 2nd Anniversary chasing the blues away through vinyl aggression.

Since the NY Times indicates that sales of 1984 by George Orwell have been going up recently for "some" reason, it seems to make sense that more people should be listening to 1984 by Bowie, 1969 by Iggy/Stooges, and maybe even in the year 2525 by Zager and Evans. Anyway, since Love is All Around whether you watch Mary Tyler Moore(*) or listen to The Troggs I reckon you can certainly drop by tomorrow 10 ish to 2ish.

SPORTSMAN'S CLUB
948 N. WESTERN AVE. CHICAGO, COOK COUNTY, STATE OF ILLINOIS, UNITED STATES OF AMERICA, CONTINENT OF

NORTH AMERICA; WESTERN HEMISPHERE; THE EARTH; THE SOLAR SYSTEM; THE UNIVERSE; THE MIND OF GOD

See http://www.oldpunksrule.com/ for my 2016 review.

Will also be debuting the latest LaCzar/Shuga Records vinyl release by Max Loebman and some other new and new/old stuff.

*Image of The Minus 5 doing a great cover of the Mary Tyler Moore theme last night.

Chapter 11: SXSW Recap (in bullet form) and Sportsman's DJ

Subject: SXSW Recap (in bullet form) and Sportsman's DJ

From: Lazar, Bart
Sent: Wed, Mar 22, 2017, 5:53 PM

Hi Everybody:

I am back from Austin and excited to share some of the new and old stuff I heard this year at Sportsman's Club, 948 Western Avenue, this Saturday from 10:00 pm to about 245 am.

I should have a bit more complete analysis later on, but it may be not really be more substantive. But I might deal with issues such as whether some bands perform better by day (and maybe sober) or is it just me? Or some of the difficulties (noted briefly below) about whether you would rather be famous for one very popular song, or disavow it in order to show the world the quality of your entire catalog, or the merits of one or two members of a band performing as that band, or is it really just a cover band. It all may be way too esoteric even for me to distill.

I'll also play from my next record release--Max Loebman--great pop.

Here are some bullet reviews of probably the 10 best

Downtown Boys--Now more than ever we need this anti-white supremacist punk group from Providence to challenge us to not be quietly complicit and move forward to do greater things within our society and thrash off our anger productively.

Duchess Says--Confrontational electro-clash dance music from Montreal. Annie Claude is one of the most dynamic frontwomen in rock, making the crowd split in two, kneel on the floor, dance on the stage, carry her on your back--whatever Duchess Says!

Modern English-Not merely a one-hit wonder --had an a great, gloomy, pulsing album on 4AD before entering pop history, but if you had to choose one, would you prefer to be remembered and compensated for I Melt With You or dark political and social commentary. See them at Empty Bottle on April 6 and decide.

Tokyo Ska Paradise Orchestra-- A nine piece Japanese band with 4 horn players belting out ska, soul, stax, soundtrack and other dance-worthy sounds. The epitome of a unique SXSW experience.

Cosmonauts--Droney stoner psych and garage don't get any better than these guys--you can see them free at the Bottle on April 3, then you can thank me!

Cheetah Chrome/Johnny Blitz--Dead Boys simulacrum--for the 40th (!) anniversary of the Dead Boys' Young, Loud and Snotty brought the Cleveland punk scene back to CBGBs showing the close connection between Led Zeppelin and punk.

Sandinistas--Delivering brash harmonic punky sounds like the Subways or Libertines, rather than the Clash as you might expect from the name, this new Welsh band combines catchy sing.

Chain of Flowers--Another positively clanging Welsh band with e

Priests--If not for Downtown Boys, this DC band would probably be on the top tier of punk bands. Playing (early in the day, I bet) at Pitchfork

Cindy Wilson--- Best known from the B-52's, she is channeling a more Madonna-esque vibe.

Here is a Spotify playlist of a bunch of the bands you might like, including those listed above.
https://open.spotify.com/user/blazar331/playlist/0TPd46coHSp93ukcc1fufM

Best cover: Ce Plane Por Moi – Crocodiles

Most Serendipitous Moment--While just walking on a residential street in E. Austin between shows, seeing the Austin Music Award's Best Austin Band Calliope Musicals in someone's backyard.

Best Tacos--Almost impossible to pick one, but this year it was Pueblo Viejo, a truck on East 6th Street.

Chapter 12: Last Night an Algorithm Saved My Life From a Broken Heart - Human DJ June 24 Sportsman's Club

Subject: Last Night an Algorithm Saved My Life From a Broken Heart - Human DJ June 24 Sportsman's Club

From: Lazar, Bart
Sent: Thu, Jun 22, 2017, 5:00 PM

As technology displaces thought and action it is important to remember what human art there is the curation process in all forms of culture.

I was reminded of this two times last month when the soundtrack of a bar suspiciously mimicked some aspects of something that I just might play. For example, at The Dawson, I heard Widowspeak, Dum Dum Girls and Fear of Men in succession---three of "MY" bands, two of whom I am proud to say I saw for the first time several years ago as opening acts at the Empty Bottle (and later at SXSW, Schuba's and Chop Shop) and the third as the headliner at Empty Bottle, Cubby Bear, Metro, Bottom Lounge SX, and more. The second night at Osteria Langhe it was Thee Oh Sees, Bleached and Deerhunter--again three favorites. It turns out that one was playing a Ty Segall channel and the other an "independents" channel on a computerized streaming service.

These services (or my playlists on Spotify!) can be great methods and potentially entertaining ways of finding out about new artists who play music that is similar to something you like--so I am glad that a bartender at Osteria can turn patrons on to steamrolling engine of Thee Oh Sees or that people chilling on the sun decks of this city might unintentionally pick up the ethereal pulse of Fear of Men----and perhaps be intrigued or inspired to learn more.

Yet, there is still something cold and formulaic about Watson's playlist, cultural gatekeeping and rules of inclusion, which by nature also exclude. And, oh, by the way where is the FEELING? This is not intended to be an essay about Bladerunner or Westworld but more about what the psalmist, Dewey Finn, presented --- "If you wanna rock, you gotta break the rules".

So next time you listen to an algorithm, or follow some other human or non-human means that uses technology to choose what you hear next--don't forget to think about what you would like to hear next and how you would do it differently. Because you should be what you play, not what you are programmed to play.

Oh yeah, so I am going to make and break (and ok, probably follow) some rules at Sportsman's Club. The patio will be open and it has a great new sound system I'm checking with my computer to see which records to bring with me this week ☺

Sportsman's Club 948 WESTERN AVE. (Augusta and Western) Saturday June 24 from a little before 10 to about 245.

If you pass by the New City kiosk on your walks about town check out my little article on one key difference between djing at a Summer festival and a club.

For those of you who can't stay out that late or want to check out me by daylight, I will be djing at Taste of Chicago on Thursday Evening July 6--I'll send another email about it and postulate some more.

Happy Pride Weekend.

Chapter 13: Sunshine, Post-Pitchfork Progressive Pop and Post Punk [Add Your Own P here] Sportsman's DJ thing tomorrow

Subject: Sunshine, Post-Pitchfork Progressive Pop and Post Punk [Add Your Own P here] Sportsman's DJ thing tomorrow

From: Lazar, Bart
Sent: Fri, Jul 28, 2017, 3:57 PM

We have made it to (or partially through) our Mid Summer's Nightmare, or if we avoid the news, our mid-Summer quick break btw Pitchfork and Lolla. This means we can let sunshine flow softly through our windows today as we meditate on which of the many wonderful things to do on this particular weekend. You can sit there a-thinking, on your velvet throne, but may I suggest an evening and night on Western, perhaps bouncing back and forth between the Empty Bottle where Chicago's best post punk band Negative Scanner is playing and Sportsman's Club, where I am playing OPM.

That is actually how I first became acquainted with Sportsmans, popping in between bands at EB shows. It can take time, I know it, but in a while the rhythm between the two places lets you commute in style.

A lot of cool new and old stuff to play ranging from Pitchfork stuff like Priests, Madame Gandhi, PJ and LCD to old stuff from a guy whose studio band united Page, Bonham and John Paul Jones in the early/mid 60's and my new LaCzar records release the Powerhaunts.

Anyway you want it, when you make your mind up your going to Sportman's Club, 948 N. Western Avenue, from a 10 - 245 (though if someone fills in I may run to EB to watch NS kill for their 30 minute set!)..

This is the age of machinery,
A mechanical nightmare,
The wonderful world of technology,
Napalm hydrogen bombs biological warfare,
This is the twentieth century,
But too much aggravation
It's the age of insanity,
What has become of the green pleasant fields of Jerusalem.
Ain't got no ambition, I'm just disillusioned
I'm a twentieth century man but I don't want to be here.
My mama said she can't understand me
She can't see my motivation
Just give me some security,
I'm You keep all your smart modern writers
Give me William Shakespeare
You keep all your smart modern painters
I'll take Rembrandt, Titian, Da Vinci and Gainsborough,
Girl we gotta get out of here
We gotta find a solution
I'm a twentieth century man but I don't want to die here.
I was born in a welfare state
Ruled by bureaucracy
Controlled by civil servants
And people dressed in grey
Got no privacy got no liberty
'cause the twentieth century people

Took it all away from me.
Don't want to get myself shot down
By some trigger happy policeman,
Gotta keep a hold on my sanity
I'm a twentieth century man but I don't want to die here.
Sir Raymond Douglas Davies 1971!

Read more: Kinks - 20th Century Man Lyrics | MetroLyrics (http://www.metrolyrics.com/20th-century-man-lyrics-kinks.html#ixzz4oA674H2r)

Chapter 14: BBB--Burgers, Booze and Bart---Sportsman's Club Sunday May 10 4-9pm

Subject: BBB--Burgers, Booze and Bart---Sportsman's Club Sunday May 10 4-9pm

From: Lazar, Bart
Sent: Wed, Sep 6, 2017, 6:30 PM

Just a short note that I am excited to be DJing this Sunday at Sportsman's Club, where you will be able to score the best in Chicago Rootstock burger, great drinks, music that bites and more on what should be a beautiful day.
And for those of you who complain about my late night sets--ahem--this is early.

"The eastern world, it is explodin',
Violence flarin', bullets loadin',
You're old enough to kill but not for votin',
You don't believe in war, but what's that gun you're totin',
And even the Jordan river has bodies floatin',
But you tell me over and over and over again my friend,
Ah, you don't believe we're on the eve of destruction.
Don't you understand, what I'm trying to say?
And can't you feel the fears I'm feeling today?
If the button is pushed, there's no running away,
There'll be no one to save with the world in a grave,

Take a look around you, boy, it's bound to scare you, boy,
And you tell me over and over and over again my friend,
Ah, you don't believe we're on the eve of destruction.
Yeah, my blood's so mad, feels like coagulatin',
I'm sittin' here, just contemplatin',
I can't twist the truth, it knows no regulation,
Handful of Senators don't pass legislation,
And marches alone can't bring integration,
When human respect is disintegratin',
This whole crazy world is just too frustratin',
And you tell me over and over and over again my friend,
Ah, you don't believe we're on the eve of destruction
Think of all the hate there is in Red China!
Then take a look around to Selma, Alabama!
Ah, you may leave here, for four days in space,
But when your return, it's the same old place,
The poundin' of the drums, the pride and disgrace,
You can bury your dead, but don't leave a trace,
Hate your next door neighbor, but don't forget to say grace,
And you tell me over and over and over and over again my friend,
You don't believe we're on the eve of destruction.
No, no, you don't believe we're on the eve of destruction
-P. F. Sloan

Chapter 15: It's a Nice Day to START AGAIN (extend dramatically)--Sportsman's Club Saturday night September 30 DJ thing --this is a correct date (and note free Eddy Clearwater concert next week!)

Subject: It's a Nice Day to START AGAIN (extend dramatically)--Sportsman's Club Saturday night September 30 DJ thing --this is a correct date (and note free Eddy Clearwater concert next week!)

From: Lazar, Bart
Sent: Fri, Sep 29, 2017, 5:50 PM

To start again--a clean slate-what a concept of atonement or ablution.

I personally fit in the "I fast to repent for sins and ideally shed a few pounds" department.

And it can really happen for everyone, regardless of religion, race, ethnicity, nationality, age, gender, gender preference, and perhaps even political ideology. Please forgive me for my naivete, but this is the time.

But time is fleeting, and the gates will be closing soon so don't let madness take control. But, if you feel like sinning, please drop by Sportsmans Club 948 n. western. Anytime from 945 to closing tomorrow Saturday the 30th.

And, next Thursday come by International House to see Eddy Clearwater, one of Chicago's living blues legends, do a free concert. Ihouse is turning 85 and Eddy is 83 I think so they are a good match. I first helped put Eddy Clearwater on at UChicago in 1979! As my first concert so it is personal for me too. Just as I may clean my slate, it is nice to revisit the gold.

This is no time for Celebration
this is no time for Shaking Heads
This is no time for Backslapping
this is no time for Marching Bands
This is no time for Optimism
this is no time for Endless Thought
This is no time for my country Right or Wrong
remember what that brought
There is no time
there is no time
There is no time
there is no time
This is no time for Congratulations
this is no time to Turn Your Back
This is no time for Circumlocution
this is no time for Learned Speech
This is no time to Count Your Blessings
this is no time for Private Gain
This is no time to Put Up or Shut Up
it won't no time to come back this way again
There is no time
there is no time

There is no time
there is no time
This is no time to Swallow Anger
this is no time to Ignore Hate
This is no time to be Acting Frivolous
because the time is getting late
This is no time for Private Vendettas
this is no time to not know who you are
Self knowledge is a dangerous thing
the freedom of who you are
This is no time to Ignore Warnings
this is no time to Clear the Plate
Let's not be sorry after the fact
and let the past become out fate
There is no time
there is no time
There is no time
there is no time
This is no time to turn away and drink
or smoke some vials of crack
This is a time to gather force
and take dead aim and Attack
This is no time for Celebration
this is no time for Saluting Flags
This is no time for Inner Searchings
the future is at head
This is no time for Phony Rhetoric
this is no time for Political Speech
This is a time for Action
because the future's Within Reach
This is the time
this is the time
This is the time
because there is no time
There is no time
there is no time

There is no time
there is no time
Lou Reed.

opening to close soon so if so before madness takes control, take control of your madness for a moment. Bshort, so think about it, and spreference.

Chapter 16: Wring In the Old and Make it New--Sportsman's Club DJ Thing--December 30

Subject: Wring In the Old and Make it New --Sportsman's Club DJ Thing--December 30

From: Lazar, Bart
Sent: Fri, Dec 29, 2017, 1:49 AM

This year I am having a bit of a hard time with the New Year's idiom ring out the old, ring in the new. Mind you--there some (maybe many) aspects of 2017 I would prefer not carry over into our new year. But at the same time, it is really important to embrace the great experiences we had in 2017 in spite of and to spite of certain abhorrent people who shall not be named. So many people have cared, marched for, loved, stood up for, protected for each other and not tolerated and demanded accountability for the abhorrent acts of others. Not just in Star Wars can great good combat great evil--we are knee deep in it.

Which is even more reason to drain every drop of lustrous liquid from that dishrag that was 2017 and turn it into a potent craft cocktail to launch you into 2018 with conviction.

I can't think of a better way than to imbibe the craft cocktails, amaro machine and/or low lifes' of Sportman's Club on the eve of the eve, while I pay some homage to great performances and sad losses of performers during the past year. Plus--see the attached to check out some of the "new" vinyl I have in store for those that dare.

Our year in review (and more) class is in session at: Sportsman's Club, 948 N. Western Avenue, Chicago, Illinois 60622
December 30, 2017 10:00-2:45

Happy New Year!!--Bart

Chapter 17: Then You Know You Must Leave the Capitol. On your way stop by Sportsman's Club Saturday January 27 (Plus Save May 26 for an Upcoming Event You won't want to miss)

Subject: Then You Know You Must Leave the Capitol. On your way stop by Sportsman's Club Saturday January 27 (Plus Save May 26 for an Upcoming Event You won't want to miss)

From: Lazar, Bart
Sent: Thu, Jan 25, 2018, 11:12 PM

In 1981 Mark E. Smith wrote about leaving the physical, geographic, mental, lifestyle or metaphorical capitol. Some might even choose to apply a different meaning today. Like anything, it is subject to interpretation at various times.

Mark left one of his and our capitols yesterday. Like many outsider artists he used imaginative ways to provoke attention and challenge norms in form and meaning of music and performance. His lyrics and "singing" (or rather ranting, singsong whine or slur/mumbling) hovered, hammered and waxed upon on subjects like over caffeination, forms of communication, political disasters, Britain's inappropriate fascination with lineage or even paying homage both to the Queen and the Kinks in one awesome cover of Victoria. Musically, too he teased with groovy bass-led dance number, hyped with post punk percussiveness or tried to force you to run out of the room with arrhythmia. A prolific, quixotic, chaotic genius to taste a bit of to see if he connects with some aspect of your sonic palate.

I will be playing more melodic Fall Saturday along with a bunch of new stuff that sounds old, old stuff that sounds new and good stuff that sounds good.

Sportsman's Club 956 N. Western Avenue. Chicago-Now (I mean Saturday).
10:00 pm (or a bit earlier if you insist) - 245 am (not a bit later even if you insist).

Programming note-I am switching to second Saturdays at Sportsmans starting in February.

Oh--and block your calendar for May 26 for a special concert by a band which was included in my New City Best of 2017 lists! More to come and I will nag you in my next 4 monthlies.

The tables covered in beer
Showbiz whines, minute detail
Its a hand on the shoulder in Leicester Square
Its vaudeville pub back room dusty pictures of
White frocked girls and music teachers
The beds too clean
The waters poison for the system

Then you know in your brain
Leave the Capitol!
Exit this Roman shell!
Then you know you must leave the capitol
Straight home, straight home, straight home

One room, one room
Then you know in your brain
You know in your brain
Leave the capitol!
Exit this Roman shell!
Then you know you must leave the capitol
Straight home, straight home, straight home
one room
Then you know in your brain
You know in your brain
Leave The Capitol
I live with cancer death wife!
Then you know you must leave the capitol

It will not drag me down
I will leave this ten times town
I will leave this fucking dump
One room, one room

Hotel maids smile in unison
Then you know in your brain
You know in your brain
Leave the Capitol
Exit this Roman shell
Then you know you must leave the capitol

I laughed at the great God Pan
I didnae, I didnae
I laughed at the great god Pan
I didnae, I didnae, I didnae, I didnae
Leave the Capitol
Exit this Roman shell.
Then you know you must leave the capitol

Pan resides in welsh green masquerades
On welsh cat caravans
But the monty
Hides in curtains

Grey blackish cream
All the paintings you recall
All the side stepped cars
All the brutish laughs
From the flat and the wild dog downstairs
Mark Edward Smith.

Chapter 18: Notice of Two/Second Weeks DJ thing Saturday February 10-Sportsman's Club

Subject: Notice of Two/Second Weeks DJ thing Saturday February 10-Sportsman's Club

From: Lazar, Bart
Sent: Wed, Feb 7, 2018, 9:41 PM

A lot can happen in two weeks, the evil empire can be defeated (at least in football), financial panic and deep, cleansing breaths of financial relief can flow (wait that was only 4 days), the government can shut down and go back and do it again (was that 4 days also?), you can go and return from vacation, play basketball 10 out of 14 days (at least I did) choose homage over hubris (even at the last minute) or not or do something good for your family, a friend, neighbor, yourself or the world and actually choose not to tell (or post it to) anyone--let's all do that in the next two weeks!

As for me, I can only hope that I left Sportsman's Club two weeks ago sonically satiated and that when I return it will be the same old, fun place filled with warmth that can only be provided by friends, friendly bartenders, great booze (artificial warmth of course) and some sort of entertainment. That's where I am the recidivist back again on two weeks break segueing into the second Saturday of each month at Sportsman's this year.

It's International Clash Day today, (2x magnificent 7=14) but every month I celebrate punk, pre and post-punk progressive pop, new wave and indie music--all vinyl. (and when is International Jam day?).

So please take a break from the snow and cold and hang out for a bit.

Sportsman's Club, 948 N. Western Avenue, Chicago, Cook County, IL 60622, United States of America, Western Hemisphere, the Earth, the part of the Solar System Elon Musk does not control; the Universe; (and for those that believe) the mind of God.
10:00- 245 Saturday February 10.

And for those that are planning. On May 26 I am proud to present ESG--the legendary Bronx-band that combined funk and no wave to create a unique dance music sound that has been incredibly influential to the hip-hop world. This will be their only stop in Chicago on their 40th anniversary tour, and I guarantee it will be memorable.

Just check this out from a show I saw at Hurrahs in 1981--Renee Scroggins still sings THAT good.
https://www.youtube.com/watch?v=MZMJX6sniE0

The show is at the excellent sounding venue--The Promontory in Hyde Park. Tickets are available here:
https://www.eventbrite.com/e/esg-tickets-42584358964

You should be there. I'll nag you. It's for your own good. Saturday Night's Alright too for Saturday's Child and all you Saturday's Kids.

Chapter 19: Cambridge Analytica Thinks I Am 32 Years Old--I Tend to Agree-- DJ Thing at LUDLOW LIQUORS-- Friday March 23

Subject: Cambridge Analytica Thinks I Am 32 Years Old--I Tend to Agree-- DJ Thing at LUDLOW LIQUORS-- Friday March 23

From: Lazar, Bart
Sent: Thu, Mar 22, 2018, 3:47 PM

We have learned that this week that if you like Tom Waits you are open minded (agreed), The Smiths you are neurotic (feh), and Judas Priest you are not agreeable (you can't win disagreeing with that!). So if you are curious how the FB/Cambridge Analytica methodology operates you can go to the University of Cambridge web site and try things out for yourself. https://applymagicsauce.com/demo.html [Editor's note: the link no longer works]. I just put in a few bands I like and typically play into the psychometric analytical tool and the attached is the result. Gee, I am a liberal and artistic, 32 year old that is the epitome of masculinity. I'm shocked, shocked to find that analytics are going on here.

Anyway, time is fleeting so I just wanted to mention that I am dj-ing at the one month anniversary for the brand new Ludlow

Liquors--a new Avondale bar with a nice vibe, awesome sound system and great drinks and food--as well as what will be a very fun backyard garden https://www.ludlow-liquors.com/ 2959 N. California from about 10-145.

Also, so I don't spam you next week. A little plug for a great, free show I am putting on at University of Chicago featuring The Secret Drum Band--with members from Explode Into Colors and !!!. There will also be a lecture on the relationship between ecology and music. That's next Thursday March 29--more details in the poster and link.
https://ihouse.uchicago.edu/events/event/documenting_ecosystems_soundscapes_and_percussion_composition/

Chapter 20: It's Never Too Late--Not Necessarily Referring to my DJ Thing Saturday April 14 at Sportsman's

Subject: It's Never Too Late--Not Necessarily Referring to my DJ Thing Saturday April 14 at Sportsman's

From: Lazar, Bart
Sent: Wed, Apr 11, 2018, 11:37 PM

Easter--it's supposed to be a sign of Spring, not snowy (or snowed-out)baseball games, but Aries birthday celebrants know the drill and temperature variation.

Just as there is substantial uncertainty to late March/early April weather, there is quite a spectrum to redemption. Maybe you are in Patti Smith's camp (Jesus died for somebody's sins, but not mine), or maybe you are in Billy Idol's (It's a nice day to START AGAIIIIIIIIN). In between black and white, you may reside in a world of gray with just a smidge of optimism--cue Ray Davies (One day we'll be free, we won't care, just you wait and see, 'Til that day can be, don't let it get you down) or maybe you like Neil Young's crawl through the wreckage (Don't let it bring you down It's only castles burning, find someone who's turning and you will come around).

However, in this moment, in these times, I sometimes think that all of these observations are a little bit singularistic. There are moments in time when we have to look beyond ourselves, beyond our time.

I look to Martin Luther King Jr., who in August 1965 (before he told us of his dream) reminded us "When the architects of our republic wrote the magnificent words of the Constitution and the Declaration of Independence (http://americanrhetoric.com/speeches/declarationofindependence.htm), they were signing a promissory note to which every American was to fall heir. This note was a promise that all [people], yes, [people of every race] would be guaranteed the "unalienable Rights" of "Life, Liberty and the pursuit of Happiness." It is obvious today that America has defaulted on this promissory note, insofar as her citizens of color are concerned. Instead of honoring this sacred obligation, America has given [minorities] a bad check, a check which has come back marked "insufficient funds." Did he say that 55 years ago or 55 minutes ago--I cannot tell.

I look at our children, Emma Gonzalez speaking volumes with a collective silence. standing up to demand that this country make good on its marker to let all of our children pursue an education and life free of violence from unwarranted weaponry focused on unimaginable targets.

I think about Maria Alyokhina of Pussy Riot speaking at her own sentencing hearing about her own country's leader: "the system that he himself created—the power vertical, where all control is carried out effectively by one person. And that power vertical is uninterested, completely uninterested, in the opinion of the masses. And what worries me most of all is that the opinion of the younger generations is not taken into consideration. We believe that the ineffectiveness of this administration is evident in practically everything." Did she say that about someone, or someone else--I cannot tell.

And I look at Victoria Ruiz of The Downtown Boys forcefully (and, I think joyfully but with a purpose) dancing and howling through the groovy bass line that she has "come to cash a check. It's a promissory note" from our society--the same as MLK's.

It's a lot for any of us to take. Me, I can offer heavy doses of vinyl therapy--after a day at the Chirp record fest- and remind you that there really is still time, but complacency is being silently complicit.. And another thing that Dr. King told us: We are now faced with the fact that tomorrow is today. We are confronted with the fierce urgency of now. In this unfolding conundrum of life and history, there "is" such a thing as being too late. This is no time for apathy or complacency. This is a time for vigorous and positive action. (and don't get me started about Lou Reed's "There is No Time").

Please act vigorously, positively and in your own special way. Care for each other and mind the gap.

Oh yeah, the vinyl therapy will commence around 10 pm and run til close (around 245 am) at Sportsman's Club, 948 N. Western Avenue, Chicago.

And, remember to put May 26 on your calendar.
http://do312.com/events/2018/5/26/esg,
https://www.newyorker.com/magazine/2018/03/05/esgs-otherworldly-sound [Editor's note: link no longer works]

[some other stuff I am up to]
https://www.sfchronicle.com/business/article/Facebook-faces-growing-government-scrutiny-in-12782652.php
https://www.cbsnews.com/news/everything-thats-going-wrong-for-facebook-right-now/

Chapter 21: Confidential Disclosure Re: DJ Gigs and ESG Show

Subject: Confidential Disclosure Re: DJ Gigs and ESG Show

From: Lazar, Bart
Sent: Wed, May 9, 2018, 11:11 PM

I understand that some folks have difficulty navigating the uncertain terrain of the current administration of indie music in the UK village/Homboldt Park/Logan Square areas of Chicago. Having spent a great deal of time in Ubers, Lyfts and taxis, I feel that I have a certain je ne sais quoi about hipster-land. I thought, perhaps that you might consider providing me with a retainer-for a number of months at a 5 or 6 figure amount. In exchange, I might be able to provide access. You know, the ultimate insight into what's going on--and I am not talking about Marvin Gaye's discography--if you know what I mean? --wink wink, nudge nudge. I won't provide receipts, time records, written reports, but I assure you, you will get your money's worth--and some. I mean how can one value insight of incalculable value? You just can't, and I know, because I just defined the transaction. I guess I am saying, like Sly and the Family Stone--There's a Riot Going On, and I don't you want to incite a riot? The Mekons have never been in a riot, but the Kaiser Chief can predict a riot.

As a riotous amuse bouche, I propose to offer my services in a public forum. I will present myself in the form of a vinyl dj located in two of the coolest locations over the next two weeks:

Saturday May 12 at Sportsman's Club 948 N. Western Avenue; 10-245; and
Friday, May 18 at Ludlow Liquors 10-145;

Where I will deliver subliminal messages to those that dare, and perceptible (i.e. above liminal) messages to those that just want to have fun and listen to great indie, post punk, punk, British invasion and somewhat dancey music without any regret at two of the best cocktail bars with two of the best outdoor patios in civilization. Not to mention midnight messages from JFK, MLK and Prince, among others.

Assuming you like what I purvey, I have set a numbered account in the Netherland Antilles, or you can just use one of my branded unmarked envelopes for retention.

Most importantly, I have enlisted one of the best dance, soul, funk, proto-punk bands--ESG-- to assist me in my endeavors on May 26 --9pm at the Promontory in Hyde Park for their 40th Anniversary -and perhaps last-- show-in Chicago. From the Bronx in 1978, Renee Scroggins has delivered some of the most street-cool vocals and sampled songs in dance music history--Moody, You're No Good, Earn It. Trust me--you gotta see them if you are in town. Tickets are still available at https://www.eventbrite.com/e/esg-tickets-42584358964.

I heard someone was going to unilaterally withdraw us from the Constution. But then I woke up. Dream on and see you in a better reality soonest.

Chapter 22: Loss and Found--- Ludlow Liquors DJ thing Friday June 15

Subject: Loss and Found--- Ludlow Liquors DJ thing Friday June 15

From: Lazar, Bart
Sent: Wed, Jun 13, 2018, 10:26 PM

Loss.

I am pretty sure we have all lost a lot recently. Whatever was lost--it is important to sense it, even if it permeates your soul for a while.

But travel with me for a moment through another dimension, where we cast the darkness of loss out of sight, sound and mind. Which stop do I disembark at ---found. You don't have to choose sides, but embrace, embolden and [choose your own e-rooted adjective for alliterative purposes] yourself with what you/we have found.

I submit for your consideration, Eddy Clearwater. I was lucky to "find" him at Kingston Mines in winter weather that cost Mayor Bilandic his job (you might ask, who goes out in the worst snowstorm in history--duh, I do, and continue to do so). Playing his right-handed guitar, left-handed and upside down, and as much Chuck Berry as BB King., he, his band, including vocalist Bad Bad Leroy Brown, knew how to take a snowstorm, sprinkle it with blues, top it off with power chords and turn what could be a calamity into magic.

Some friends and I had a crazy idea to throw the wildest party ever at University of Chicago, and outside of the Checkerboard Lounge we hit up Eddy to be our headliner, and he agreed--for a mere $500 and a bottle of Jack Daniels. Between Eddy, an Everclear spiked punch and a mass light up of something or other at 11:11 pm, the place where fun went to die was exhumed, just for one day.

I would catch Eddy around town or at his club Reservation Blues on Milwaukee Ave (where Revel Room is today). Whether he was just a bit ahead or behind the times, it is hard to tell, but as many sets as he would perform each night, he always rocked the house with a smile. You can ask me for the long story, but recently, I was lucky to bring him, IN HIS 80S back to UChicago for a couple of shows. As an elder statesman of the blues, his performances seemed more rooted in the traditional, than his more rock and roll sets of the past. Amazingly, he could still play guitar behind his head and had become a powerful singer, belting out songs like "Too old to be married, too young to be buried."

Eddy Clearwater, a blues hall of famer, father, inspiration and more than I will ever know-- I mourn our loss of Eddy, but don't think of how he died--remember how he lived!

Remember what you have found and all that you will find!--and don't forget to smile.

You can find me Friday, June 15 at Ludlow Liquors playing a bunch of vinyl that I have found along the way.

2959 North California, from about 10 to close (around 1:30). Ludlow has an awesome patio, drinks and Filipino-infused food. I might have a special guest too.

Chapter 23: Its Not Far or Hard to Reach--Escape to Sportsman's Club--Sat July 14

Subject: Its Not Far or Hard to Reach-- Escape to Sportsman's Club--Sat July 14

From: Lazar, Bart
Sent: Thu, Jul 12, 2018, 12:57 AM

We can all hitch a ride to Rockaway Beach.

Sure, hitching is illegal, each of the Ramones are not physically with us for the journey, and since a large stretch of the beach is closed this Summer due to erosion, even the physical destination is not all there. But, ultimately, we are talking about the proverbial ride. The fact is, THE SUN IS OUT, AND I WANT SOME. Don't you?

Escapism. Is it a natural tendency or a current inexorable need? Do we, as Marx might claim, feel alienated from our product, work, community (ahem, country), or, spirit-forbid, ourselves, that we want to head to that beach? Which is probably why Corona's "find your beach" campaign is so effective. Yet, we need to take a step back and try and discern, is it the escape or the destination that is so primal and crucial to what road we choose to take?

If you follow Weil/Mann as channeled through the Animals, it is that "We Gotta Get Out of This Place"--the exit strategy is the key. Escape is the ultimate thing to do, if it is that last thing we ever do. But in that song, does anyone care about the destination? Is it really irrelevant? We can't do any better, so we better get out of this dirty old part of the city where the sun refuses to shine, as fast as we can. But what happens if we do that? Does our selfish escape make the world better? What happens if where we go sucks just as much? What is the difference between the roads? Do we move to Canada and have a nice life? Maybe.

What is a nice life, anyhow? And, what is it with all of these questions?

We can certainly pull out of this life to "win." And, as a strategic problem solver, I am not saying that for some of us that may be the most viable strategy to implement. But, naïve optimist and utopian that I am, I think that if we hitch a ride or take the A train to Rockaway Beach, we are not escaping to simply ride out to case the promised land and to settle there. Most of us are going out to exercise or freedom, have a temporary blast and will eventually take the A train or Uber home.

Returning after an emotional escapist intermezzo, we are hopefully re-energized, and not too hung over, to continue to enthusiastically take on our responsibilities, including the current and compelling mandate to care for each other repair the fabric of our communities and fight hate to re-establish a caring world through, among other things, social action and social justice.

So please get out there, hitch that ride and find that beach. Selfishly, we need you back refreshed.

The patio at Sportsman's Club is an amazing beach, worthy of your consideration, since it is filled with friendly spirits of the human and liquid kind. I find myself privileged to provide the soundtrack for such a non-judgmental space this Saturday, July 14, starting from 10-midnight with the awesome patio rocking, and until closing indoors, in a more intimate space, but still driven by punk, post punk, garage, psych, soul and other community building and authority challenging exclusively vinyl sounds. Come by and hear something new, something old, something that will make you move, and people you will want to talk to and listen to music with, maybe even me.

Sportsman's Club- 948 N. Western Avenue--(Augusta and Western)---from about 10 (seriously, I will start early on popular request) to about 245.

-Bart.

Chapter 24: Friday Reading-That Summer Feeling at Ludlow Liquors DJ thing Tonight 10pm.

Subject: Friday Reading-That Summer Feeling at Ludlow Liquors DJ thing Tonight 10pm.

From: Lazar, Bart
Sent: Fri, Aug 17, 2018, 8:27 AM

A little late notice, I know, but I took a break from writing my own DJ rants to writing one for my friends at Middlebrow Beer, which just released this morning. Please click to imbibe my continued warped exploration of escapism in these times and drop on by Ludlow Liquors for a taste of Summer's past, present and future. -Bart

middle brow: citizen how.*

*reprinted with permission

drink good. do better. find your windmill.

in every summer we look to escape from our ordinary lives to have new experiences OR JUST PLAIN CHILL OUT. i don't know about you but food and drink represent a substantial part of my summer escapes, whether it's a barbecue with friends, an event in the backyard of one or more of my favorite establishments, a trip to a place or region known for unique things to ingest, or roaming a street or music fest.

in this summer of our discontent, more perhaps than any other, we feel the urgent impulsive undertow towards diversion—that need to get out before our time is due—to chase and grasp some aspect of the promise that we made to ourselves and/or others—what do we work so hard for anyway. there is no doubt we deserve the break and are entitled to it. yet, in vacating our regular lives, i suggest that we are not playing a game of stare eyes where we simply break away from what we know is staring us right in the face.

i submit for your consideration that it is crucial not to disengage completely. though nothing will drive all of it away, we can beat the disrepair of our world and the fraying fabric of fundamental human interaction forever and ever. to do so, we gotta incorporate some reweaving as an aspect of our getaway—even as we pull away for sanity's sake. there is too much at stake.

cervantes tells us that all sorrows are less with bread, and I say I'll take mine in liquid form. which somehow brings me to middle brow beer, of all things. corona has had success with its slogan "find your beach" which provides ivory-snow-pure (i.e. 99.9%) escapism. just go ahead sit on your beach chair and crack open a beer. you can ignore the world, but you don't need a fortune cookie or an acid flashback to the 70's to know you'll never find gold on a sandy beach. so, i say don't be an ostrich, at least not this year.

middle brow's "drink good. do better" mission statement is more apropos for these treacherous times. while i'm not sure if the statement is grammatically correct, the fact that pete and his partners give 50% of their profits to charities is one of the things that drew me to the product in the first place (along with drop leaf dinners, which has combined unique dining experiences with charitable efforts). the second fact is that *mb* makes > fucking good, original beers with idiosyncratic names obliquely referencing rock and roll bands. so you get substance + form + that something extra building community.

it is important to look at doing better from the perspective of both the means of production as well as consumption. it is comforting to know that you can drink a summery kolsch beer, and in doing so support a 46-year-old independent business like gene's sausages—which was started by two Polish immigrants—all while supporting a local charities with mb's portion of the profits. as consumers, we have the power of self-determination through our commerce. so, while our opportunity to exercise our vote at the ballot does not come frequently, we have daily opportunities to vote our conscience with our wallet.

that is one of the great things about chicago's service industry community. it is a competitive market seeking to pry our hard-earned dollars in exchange for food, beverage, entertainment, and, yes, that escape. but we can really be proud that so many members of our local community get together to support each other as well as so many good cause. i urge you to look around at other products and experiences that can provide you with unique experiences, great food, drink and company, but do good. look, for example at pilot light. i have no connection to jason hammel, other than lula has been one of my and my daughters' favorite restaurants for a long time. but through pilot light, he and others have found a means to help children make healthier choices by connecting the lessons they learn in their classrooms to the foods they eat on their lunch trays, at home and in their communities. that is one way to pay it forward to help the next generation.

or if you are more comfortable with committing time over money, consider getting a group together to volunteer packing at the greater chicago food depository. if any of you let mb know of your interest in participating, i'm certain that a unique, fun, synergistic event benefitting the community will flower from your interest. or look for something your friends are doing or that meets your own personal challenges or interests—i'm certain you can find a match. and, yes, there are apps for that, too.

you don't have to read *east of eden* to comprehend the profundity of individual responsibility, the exercise of free will and its impact on lives and communities, though it does make a great summer "beach" read! we can DO BETTER. And there is nothing wrong about DRINKING (or eating) GOOD while we are at it.

drink good. do better.

Chapter 25: I Am Part of the Resistance to the Effort to End Summer. Three September DJ Things, including the Rootstock Sunday Afternoon BBQ (hello-early show!)

Subject: I Am Part of the Resistance to the Effort to End Summer. Three September DJ Things, including the Rootstock Sunday Afternoon BBQ (hello-early show!)

From: Lazar, Bart
Sent: Thu, Sep 6, 2018, 8:31 PM

Summer does not end until we say so! I wish I had the power to end other things.

But, at least thanks to global shifting, global warming or fake science without any support in fact I can wield my ESPN or something to enable me to enable you to sweat it out on the streets of September in Chicago. And, luckily for me I own a lot more songs about Summer than I do about Autumn (though when it's time, I do admit to loving to play Dave Van Ronk's Urge for Going about winter closing in). I urge you to spend your bonus Summer hours wisely. Enjoy the sun, the rain, the park and other things and maybe some of it with me. If not at Riotfest (Douglas Park 9/14-16), Negative Scanner (Empty Bottle 9/13) or praying for redemption (various places at various times for various individuals and collectives), then your best bets are at Sportsman's Club or Ludlow Liquors.

Sportsmans, this Saturday 10-close (948 North Western)

Ludlow Liquors Friday September 14, from when I get there from Riotfest (10?) to close. (2959 N. California)

Sportsmans Sunday September 16 **from 4-7 pm** at the last and best Sportsman's BBQ of the year where we will be feted with Rootstock's best of Chicago burger and more together with vinyl from me and Miss Alex White (7-9). For this one--no late night excuses!

Even this Summer--Get it While You Can.
That summer feeling.
When there's things to do not because you gotta
When you run for love not because you oughta
When you trust your friends with no reason, nada [great rhymes Jonathan!]
The joy I've named shall not be tamed

And that summer feeling is gonna haunt you one day in your life

When the cool of the pond makes you drop down on it
When the smell of the lawn makes you flop down on it
When the teenage car gets the cop down on it

That time is here
For one more year.
And that summer feeling is gonna haunt you one day in your life

If you've forgotten what I'm naming
You're gonna long to reclaim it one day

Because that summer feeling is gonna haunt you one day in your life
And if you wait until your older
A sad resentment will smolder one day
And then that summer feeling is gonna haunt you
And that summer feeling's gonna taunt you
And then that summer feeling is gonna hurt you one day in your life

When even fourth grade starts looking good
Which you hated
And first grade's looking good too
Overrated
And you boys long for some little girl that you dated
Do you long for her or for the way you were?
That summer feeling is gonna haunt you the rest of your life

When the Oldsmobile has got the top down on it
When the catamaran has got the drop down on it
When the flat of the land has got the crop down on it
Some things look good before and some things never were
But that summer feeling is gonna haunt you one day in your life

Well when your friends are in town and they got time for you
When you and them are hanging around and they don't ignore you
When you say what you will
And they still adore you
If that's not appealing, it's that summer feeling
That summer feeling is gonna haunt you one day in your life

It's gonna haunt you
It's gonna taunt you
You're gonna want this feeling inside one more time
It's gonna haunt you
It's gonna taunt you
You're gonna want this feeling inside one more time

When you're hanging around the park with the water fountain
And there's the little girl with the dirty ankles
But she's on the swings where all the dust is kicking up
And you remember the ankle locket
And the way she flirted with you
For all this time how come?
Well that summer feeling is gonna haunt you one day in your life
You'll throw away everything for it

When the playground that just was all dirt comes haunting
And that little girl that called you a flirt
Memory comes taunting
You pick these things apart, they're not that appealing
You put them together and you'll get a certain feeling
That summer feeling is gonna haunt you one day in your life

Chapter 26: What Goes Around Comes Around? Vinyl, Of Course! Sportsman's Club Sat. 10/13, Ludlow Liquors 10/19

Subject: What Goes Around Comes Around? Vinyl, Of Course! Sportsman's Club Sat. 10/13, Ludlow Liquors 10/19

From: Lazar, Bart
Sent: Wed, Oct 10, 2018, 11:56 PM

Yeah, my blood's so mad, feels like coagulatin'
I'm sittin' here, just contemplatin',
I can't twist the truth, it knows no regulation,
Handful of Senators don't pass legislation,
And marches alone can't bring integration,
When human respect is disintegratin',
This whole crazy world is just too frustratin'.
-PF Sloan

How does one change, rearrange and repair this world at this time? -me

We can chase our own self-interest, but it is
Just a matter of time, till you run out of breath
Money mountains you climb, never hedging your bets

But your luck can run out, you'd better watch your step
Just a matter of time --
- John Melville Lee Archer / Douglas James Falconer / John Albert Howard / Robert David Miles / Barry John Joseph Palmer / Mark Jeremy Seymour / Jeremy Stuart Smith / Michael Bernard Wate-- a/k/a UB40

Let's start with individual acts of kindness, justice and righteousness (hopefully our countries can agree on at least some of what those things are). We all have a stake in the betterment of our world and as well as that of those that might follow.
--me and the Talmud.

How can people have no feelings
How can they ignore their friends
Easy to be proud
Easy to say no
Especially people who care about strangers
Who care about evil and social injustice
Do you only care about being proud
How about I need a friend, I need a friend
- Galt MacDermot, James Rado, Gerome Ragni--that's from Hair, though you might remember Three Dog Night.

I can only speak for me but I think that for that portion of America that I am a part of, it is a combination of individual and collective action is meaningful. The opposite is apathy and inaction.
-me.

"Our lives begin to end the day we become silent about things that matter."

In the past apathy was a moral failure.
Today it is a form of moral and political suicide.
This is no time for apathy or complacency.
This is a time for vigorous and positive action.

-Martin Luther King

This is no time to Swallow Anger
this is no time to Ignore Hate
This is no time to be Acting Frivolous
because the time is getting late
This is no time for Private Vendettas
this is no time to not know who you are
Self knowledge is a dangerous thing
the freedom of who you are
This is no time to Ignore Warnings
this is no time to Clear the Plate
Let's not be sorry after the fact
and let the past become our fate
This is no time to turn away and drink
or smoke some vials of crack
This is a time to gather force
and take dead aim and Attack
This is no time for Celebration
this is no time for Saluting Flags
This is no time for Inner Searchings
the future is at head
This is no time for Phony Rhetoric
this is no time for Political Speech
This is a time for Action
because the future's Within Reach
-Lou Reed

The biggest threat to our democracy ...
is not one individual,
it is not one big super PAC billionaires…
It is apathy, it is indifference, it is us not doing what we are supposed to do.
-Barack Obama

I won't tell you what you are supposed to do. I can tell you what you know--there is much to do.

I can tell you that I registered at Chicagocares.org to sign up for volunteer activities. You might find something that you, your family, your friends, your pet may want to do to help others, yourself and our world. I didn't need Taylor Swift to tell me to register to vote neither (though I appreciate her effort).

And, while it may not be entirely altruistic, I think most of those quoted above would be ok with you dropping by Sportsmans Club, this Saturday 10/13 and/or Ludlow Liquors 10/19 to help re-build, change and rearrange the world through three minute songs, camaraderie, conversation and excellent cocktails just shut the f**k up for a minute and comfortably enjoy the stuff I am playing.

Look what's happening out in the streets
Got a revolution (got to revolution)
Hey, I'm dancing down the streets
Got a revolution (got to revolution)
Oh, ain't it amazing all the people I meet?
Got a revolution (got to revolution)
One generation got old
One generation got soul
This generation got no destination to hold
Pick up the cry
Hey, now it's time for you and me
Got a revolution (got to revolution)
Hey, come on now we're marching to the sea
Got a revolution (got to revolution)
Who will take it from you, we will and who are we?
Well, we are volunteers of America (volunteers of America)
Volunteers of America (volunteers of America)

-Marty Balin / Paul Kantner

Chapter 27: That I Just Don't Know -Nov. DJ

Subject: That I Just Don't Know -Nov. DJ

From: Lazar, Bart
Sent: Thu, Nov 8, 2018, 11:55 PM

And I Guess

We made it through Election Day less scathed. I hope you all heeded the words of Faithless that "inaction is a weapon of mass destruction" and voted whether or not you told or showed anyone on social media. So as we enter that tunnel of darkness Chicagoans call Autumn and Winter--I submit that there is a whiter shade of gray gripping our palette's edge

We all have the ability to turn events a particular way rather than turn away from events. Whether we turn, and if so, how we turn, is not just about the seasons, Pete Seeger, Bob Dylan and Roger McGuinn, but more like Abraham, Martin and John and our far too many Americans lost through violence that can and should be curbed.

So yeah--grab that knife--but to mix, spread and create. That's the time we'll love the best.

I don't know just where I'm going, with this

But we can try for community if we can
Coz it will help us feel like we're more hu-man.
Maybe that will be the new kind of kick for us, something we ain't had.
We can make big decisions.
Change our evil ways and shit.
What would you pay, to make the hate go away?

So take a break from all those politicians making crazy sounds,*

And come hear my super crazy vinyl sounds at

- Sportsmans Club--#5 of Time Out's Best Bars in Chicago--this Saturday November 10 10 pm to close.
- Ludlow Liquors--#14 of Time Out's Best Bars in Chicago and finalist for the Jean Banchet Award for Culinary Excellence for Best Bar --Friday November 15 --10 pm-Close
- Reed's Local--The Official Club Foot Reunion (I'm on 1:10-1:50, but come earlier to hear some of the great Club Foot djs!

*With apologies to Lou, Lux, Ivy and Lana, Carrie, Corin, Janet and you.

Chapter 28: WORDS COUNT, EXPERIENCE COUNTS, THE COUNT COUNTS-- DJ Thing at Sportsman's Club this Saturday, 12/8

Subject: WORDS COUNT, EXPERIENCE COUNTS, THE COUNT COUNTS-- DJ Thing at Sportsman's Club this Saturday, 12/8

From: Lazar, Bart
Sent: Wed, Dec 5, 2018, 11:52 PM

Think about how the Count from Sesame Street attacks the mundane task of counting in an enthusiastic and innovative way. In one episode he teaches how you can count in many different ways (1. Loud, 2. Soft, 3. High, 4 Low , 5 Slow, 6. Fast.).

In looking back on this year, I know it seems like the issues that trouble us are so far away and beyond our reach.

Yet, every day we can block and tackle the fabric of community. There are so many ways that we can show 1. Ourselves, 2, others we encounter every day that we know; 3 others we encounter every day that we don't know; 4 communities, 5 governmental organizations , 6 non-governmental organizations; 7, our

environment, 8 the future world, 9 spirits that may or may not exist--- that tiny is not us. And, if asked in what ways, I suppose treating others with respect, being transparent and (mostly) truthful, speaking or acting for those that are unable to fend for themselves, and in firm, lawful, opposition to the other are the first critical and fundamental building blocks that come into mind, to as someone I once disagreed with once meant, to be a loyal friend, leave our home, our neighborhood and town better than we found it.
Like the Count, or Mary Tyler Moore, we can take a mundane task and suddenly make it all seem worthwhile.

One genre of experiences that make me think we can make it after all tends to involve music performance. Let me count some of my favorite performances of 2018 so far.

"Older" Performers

Buddy Guy/Eddy Clearwater (Buddy Guys)
Dead Boys (Beat Kitchen)
Bush Tetras (West Fest)
Fleshtones (Beat Kitchen)
ESG (Promontory)
Gary Numan (Riotfest)
Jerry Lee Lewis (Riotfest)
MC 50 (Metro)
This is Not This Heat (Pitchfork)
Angels and Devils (Hungry Brain)
PIL (Thalia Hall)

"Newer" Performers

Priests (Logan Square Arts Festival)
Diet Cig (Bottom Lounge)
Thee Oh Sees (Thalia Hall, Empty Bottle)
Negative Scanner (Empty Bottle)
Shopping (Beat Kitchen)
Follakzoid (Empty Bottle)

Algiers (Ribfest--of all places)
Kikagaku Moyo (Revolution Oktoberfest)
Summer Cannibals (Subterranean-Downstairs)
BoyGenius (Thalia Hall)

And one more experience to consider is dropping by Sportsman's Club this Saturday December 8 to listen to some of these great bands on vinyl, talk to friends and build our community.

Just remember to embrace the goal, but not the cause.

Happy Holidays and an individually and collectively meaningful New Year.

Sportsman's Club
948 N. Western (Western and Augusta)
Starting at 10.

Chapter 29: We can dream of things that someday will be- Hey it's just another DJ thing- January 12 - Sportsman's Club

Subject: We can dream of things that someday will be- Hey it's just another DJ thing- January 12 - Sportsman's Club

From: Lazar, Bart
Sent: Wed, Jan 9, 2019, 10:47 PM

Dreams.

Is there another word that can make you turn your head on an angle like a curious dog propelling your mind off its boosters -- journeying from crayons to perfume and beyond?

I submit that we can still dream of things that have never been-- but someday will be. (♥Mekons).

May this be the year that we can live in a nation where people are not judged by any characteristic, but by the content of their character (≤Martin Luther King Jr).

May this be the year where dreams planted in discontent rise into fruition from action. (Me)

If you dare to struggle, you dare to win (Fred Hampton)

Let this be the year you catch your dreams before they slip away,
coz if you lose your dreams you will lose your mind
(Richards/Jagger)

We don't need to choose between Texas medicine or railway gin.
Like a dream, we are not what we seem
Let's write the sky with letters, only love can live in our dream
(Black/London/Bowie)

Find the time, the place, the people, the thing.
Speaking of the thing, I'll take time off from (or time on for)
dreaming to take you there coz I gotta do my thing this Saturday:

At Sportsman's Club (#6 on best bars in Chicago-Time Out among other deserving accolades),
948 N. Western (Western and Augusta). 10-late. 50+ years of vinyl and dreams.

Chapter 30: Declaration of (Dis) Interest-- Sportsman's Club Saturday February 9

Subject: Declaration of (Dis) Interest-- Sportsman's Club Saturday February 9

From: Lazar, Bart
Sent: Wed, Feb 6, 2019, 11:01 PM

In the course of human events, cunning, ambitious and unprincipled people subvert the power of the people and usurp for themselves the reins of government. The question then becomes whether a person can stand adversity.

It is in the everyday affairs of life that we show the qualities of practical intelligence of courage, of hardihood, and endurance, and above all the power of devotion to a lofty ideal, which made great the individuals who founded our nation.

The enemies one makes are one way in which you can judge a person, but you can also test a person's character by providing her or him with power. Those tests failed and those enemies with whom we can relate can tell you a lot!

There is somethin' left to lose--freedom is never more than one generation away from extinction. We didn't pass it to our children in the bloodstream. It must be fought for, protected and handed on to them to do the same.

If we tell our children they will forget, if we teach our children they may remember--but involve our children and they will learn. So involve your children well and maybe their parent's hell will quickly go by. We should not be cursing the darkness, but lighting a candle that can guide us thru the darkness to a safe and sane future.

It is for none and all of these reasons that I have decided today to not seek election as President of the United States. I will throw my support to anyone that has the capacity to understand and hold self-evident truths--or maybe potato, or baby corn for that matter--baby corn is really cute and deserves your support!

Maybe it is comforting to remember that what kills a skunk is the publicity it gives itself. And that no person has a good enough memory to be a successful liar.

But remember, remember always that all of us, and you and I especially, are descended from immigrants and revolutionists.

Tom, George, Teddy, Abe, Kris, Ron, Ben, Graham and John will be joining me in spirits this Saturday February 9 at Sportsman's Club- just ranked the 38th best bar in the United States by the Daily Meal while I teach and involve those present in suggesting alternative realities through a mélange of vinyl that is old, new and somehow both.

I will be Pres-ent at Sportsman's Club, 948 N. Western Avenue 10-late.

Chapter 31: Low Expectations Exceeded vs. High Expectations Met--Discuss or Experience at Sportsman's Club This Saturday.

Subject: Low Expectations Exceeded vs. High Expectations Met--Discuss or Experience at Sportsman's Club This Saturday.

From: Lazar, Bart
Sent: Thu, Mar 7, 2019, 1:04 AM

Cultural pseudo-intellectual that I am, I often espouse a theory related to enjoyment that goes like this.

Let's say you love a band and have high expectations about a concert. The concert is great and meets expectations.

Compare that with a situation where you go with a friend or otherwise see a band you do not know or have low expectations. The concert is good or great and exceeds expectations.

Which is the more enjoyable experience? Does the surprise factor triumph over a met expectation.

Tonight, while talking to an esteemed colleague (ok it was my Uber driver) I came up with a variation for those of you that are more into sports.

Let's say the Jordan-era Bulls are playing a team you expect them to beat--and they do, handily.

Compare that with a situation where the Rose-era or Rondo-era (however short) Bulls are playing a team you expect them to lose to--but they gut out a close win;

Which is the more enjoyable experience?

I am not sure if there is a right answer but it is sort of fun to argue the "absolute" score of the experience perceived vs. the "net" score between expectation and delivery.

Or maybe an experience is just supposed to be what it is, not quantified in any type of supposedly objective way.

So, gather ye experiences while ye may--including coming bye Thee Olde Sportsman's Club on Saturday March 9 so that you can cobble together the tastes of creative craft cocktails, the sights of Saturday night at one of the coolest bars in Chicago and the pre and post-punk and indie sounds purveyed by yours truly.

Guaranteed to meet or exceed any expectations.

Sportsman's Club, 948 N. Western Avenue. 10 pm to close.

Chapter 32: Record Store Night -- Saturday April 13 at Sportsman's Club--Free Concerts, SX mini review and So Much More!

Subject: Record Store Night -- Saturday April 13 at Sportsman's Club--Free Concerts, SX mini review and So Much More!

From: Lazar, Bart
Sent: Thu, Apr 11, 2019, 11:51 PM

There is so much on my head that I just have to stick to the objective facts, just the facts man/maa'm--not sure who else is capable of that any more in an unredacted form (oops I strayed into commentary/failed already).

1) Yes. I am djing Saturday, April 13 at Sportsman's Club, located at 948 N. Western Avenue, Chicago, Illinois, 60622--from ~10pm -245 Central Time.
2) Yes. I am playing only vinyl. I have a lot of great new stuff that sounds old, and old stuff that sounds new.
3) Yes. I saw/heard some great bands at SXSW--Gurr power pop/punk from Berlin, The Beths harmonic indie pop, from New Zealand, Pottymouth punky from LA (formerly from MA), Ratboys Americana from Chicago, Bush Tetras funk/punk from 1979 NYC, Viagra Boys deep hard rock

groove from Stockholm, Fontaines DC talky, gritty driven post punk from Dublin, Haelos, trip hop dance from London, Illuminati Hotties emo indie punk from LA, Pip Blom jangly pop from Amsterdam; Priests punky confrontational garage rock from DC (see Priests and Gurr in Chicago April 22) , Katie Harkin earthy, emotional groovey rock from Leeds, The Crazy World of Arthur Brown--yes the guy that brought you Fire in 1968 (yes, it was him, and yes he was wild and great), .Chia--shiny dance pop from Nagoya, Japan; Ezra Collection, horn led jazz darlings of London, The Comet is Coming, a sax-led freaky funk jazz space band from London, ok the OH Sees breakaway train now based in LA. And, yes, I will play some of these bands on Saturday.

4) Yes-- please see Dengue Fever play at International House, 1414 E. 59th Street, on Thursday May 2, at 7 FOR FREE. Dengue Fever is an amazing Cambodian/American indie rock band. (if you don't believe me check out rave reviews on NPR, NY Times, etc. or listen at https://denguefevermusic.com/ The show is free, just rsvp to me!-
5) Yes--please see Negative Scanner on Saturday at 3 pm at Reckless on Milwaukee--that is free too.
6) Yes--please see my friends from Denmark The Foreign Resort, at Beat Kitchen next Wednesday April 17. It won't be free, but will be worth it to see the only dark wave dance band that ever played in my living room!.
7) No. I won't stop trying to influence the cultural lives of others, particularly those I care about.

Yes Yes It will be fine.
We are sick and tired
Of being promised this and that.
We work all day, we sweat and slave
To keep the wealthy fat.
They fill our heads with promises

And bamboozle us with facts,
Then they put on false sincerity
Then they laugh behind our backs.

Money and Corruption
Are ruining the land
Crooked politicians
Betray the working man,
Pocketing the profits
And treating us like sheep,
And we're tired of hearing promises
That we know they'll never keep.

Promises, promises, all we get are promises.
Show us a man who'll understand us, guide us and lead us.

We are sick and tired
Of having to ask them cap in hand
We crawl on the floor
We beg for more,
But still we are ignored.
We're tired of being herded
Like a mindless flock of sheep
And we're tired of hearing promises
That we know they'll never keep.

We've got to stand together
Every woman, every man,
Because money and corruption are ruining the land.
Show us a man who'll be our Saviour and will lead us.
Show us a man who'll understand us, guide us and lead us.
Show us a man.
Workers of the nation unite.
Workers of the nation unite.

I visualise a day when people will be free
And we'll be living in a new society.
No class distinction, no slums or poverty

I have a vision of a new society.
And every home will have a stereo and TV,
A deep freeze, quadrasonic and a washing machine.
So workers of the nation unite.

I am your man
I'll work out a five-year plan
So vote for me brothers
And I will save this land
And we will nationalise the wealthy companies
And all the directors will be answerable to me,
There'll be no shirking of responsibilities
So people of the nation unite.

Union Man I'll work with you hand in hand
For we're all brothers to our Union Man.
I am your man,
Oh God how I love this land,
So join together save the Fatherland.

I visualize a day when people will be free
And we'll be living in a new society.
No class distinction, no slums or poverty,
So workers of the nation unite,
Workers of the nation unite,
People of the nation unite.
--Sir Raymond Douglas Davies --**1973**

Chapter 33: It Is All Too Easy to Say No ---It Doesn't Change Anything-- MLK Jr. --- A Summer Rant in Advance of My Sportsman's DJ Thing-This Saturday July 13.

Subject: It Is All Too Easy to Say No ---It Doesn't Change Anything-- MLK Jr. --- A Summer Rant in Advance of My Sportsman's DJ Thing-This Saturday July 13.

From: Lazar, Bart
Sent: Thu, Jul 11, 2019, 12:28 AM

Timuel D. Black Jr. is older than the temperature today-100 1/2 years old- and a pro-active witness to our history. Although a storm may be threatening our very lives today, he remains a scarce world resource to be sought out in person or in any form of media and is not gonna fade away.

Among other things, he fought for our country in WW II and has seen fire sweepin the streets of Europe and our very streets today. He simultaneously fought and fights racism, helped bring Dr. King to and desegregate jazz clubs in Chicago and has helped to build shelter in the form of numerous groundbreaking political achievements arising from our streets. He became enamored with Dr. King and saw how violence is just a shot away. He is a living reminder that "Darkness cannot drive out darkness, only light can do that. Hate cannot drive out hate, only love can do that, " that we must at some point "take a position that is neither safe, nor politic, nor popular, but ..must be taken because conscience tells [us] it is right" and "The time is always right to do what is right."

In this, the third Summer of our discontent, it may not be politic or popular but there is something to be said for seeking to achieve a common goal of stemming the flood that's threatening. Say "yes" to create some shelter, which may yet require emerging from our otherwise protective coverings --advancing a positive vision rather than getting lost in despair or apathy or being pulled so low as to hate and not achieve change and end hunger, poverty, racism, militarism and so many other isms of disparity being wrought today. Whether personal and/or political, we must understand that love is just a kiss away and remember that hatred and violence is no more than a shot away.

So, people "If you can't fly then run, if you can't run then walk, if you can't walk then crawl, [and, if you can't do any of those things take an Uber--but please don't take a scooter] but whatever you do you have to keep moving forward" and don't look back. And always remember that positive change-includes heading over to Sportsman's Club this Saturday from 10 to --closing for my monthly array of 55 + years of rock and roll vinyl. The backyard will be open til almost midnight so you can enjoy post punk outside.

Sportsman's Club
948 North Western
10 (maybe even earlier upon request) -245.
Apologies and regards to Drs. Black, King, Jagger and Richards.

Chapter 34: Build or Destroy? - Sportsman's Club August 10, 2019 10:00 on.

Subject: Build or Destroy? - Sportsman's Club August 10, 2019 10:00 on.

From: Lazar, Bart
Sent: Wed, Aug 7, 2019, 11:29 PM

It is so easy to destroy.

When I rehabbed houses I loved to do demolition. Knocking walls down, taking a crowbar to cut the strings from a sink to the wall. It's a form of freedom. Yet it took seconds of my time to take something down--it took seconds.

Seemed like some form of freedom (until I had to clean up).

It is so much harder to build. Forward thinking, attention to detail-taping, spackling, sanding, painting, repeat--boring! It took hours, and felt like some form of unrewarding bondage.

It is so much easier to criticize.

I remember my professor Roberto Mangabeira Unger advance critical legal theory, attacking all of our socio-political assumptions and how our justice system was a beautiful house built on a weak foundation, that would ultimately crash. My friends and I marveled at the way he dismissed everything we knew, while wearing designer ties that were the same color as his shirts.

Yeah, you can spit in the face of institutions, but it is so much harder to formulate a strategic plan or take action. Unger recently noted that "without prophesy and without vision politics is nothing." That means something to me in this the 50th anniversary of the first walk on the moon. Kennedy was prophetic and visionary and our country (yes, in competition with Russia) devoted virtually everything we had to meet that vision--to build unbelievable technology, to take risks.

Unger posited in 2011 that the way politics and culture are organized you have to wait for a crisis, like a meteor .Suddenly we become awake and then go to sleep again. At least HE believes that a democracy will wake up in the face of that type of danger.

I know it makes you wanna run away, wanna get away.

It hurts to stay, it hurts to go away.

It's those times that we feel so weak that we want to explode.

But when you take that moment into your hand--which should you do?.

I urge you to stay, just a little bit longer. Please stay, just a little bit more.

I think about how beachgoers form human chains to save drowning swimmers--in Panama City Beach two weeks ago and in 2017, on Lake Michigan last year.

We can build amazing things, together.

We can be together and build this Saturday night at Sportsman's Club, listening to music that challenges, builds, seeks to destroy or may be just about having fun--remember it is still ok to have fun!.

All vinyl, all the time. 948 N. Western Avenue, Chicago, Cook County, Illinois, United State of America, Continent of North

America, Western Hemisphere of the Earth, the Solar System, the Universe, the Mind of God.

This Saturday, August 10. 10 pm til they shut me down at 245.

All day
Hiding from the sun
Waiting for the golden one
Waiting for your fame
After the parade has gone
Outside was a happy place
Every face had a smile like the golden face
For a second
Your knuckles white as your fingers curl
The shot that was heard around the world
For a seconds
It took seconds of your time to take his life
It took seconds
It took seconds of your time to take his life
It took seconds
It took seconds of your time to take his life
It took seconds of your time to take his life
Seconds
Seconds
It took seconds of your time to take his life
It took seconds
It took seconds of your time to take his life
It took seconds
For a second
It took seconds of your time to take his life
It took seconds
It took seconds of your time to take his life
It took seconds
For a second
It took seconds of your time to take his life
Seconds of your time to take his life
For a second

For a second
For a second
(Yes, the Human League).

Chapter 35: There's a Riot (Fest) Going On. Join me at Sportsman's Club Saturday After.

Subject: There's a Riot (Fest) Going On. Join me at Sportsman's Club Saturday After.

From: Lazar, Bart
Sent: Thu, Sep 12, 2019, 10:26 PM

Time is fleeting this week, so I'm taking control of my madness before Riotfest takes its toll.

In talking about riots (or more apt, rock show dance floors) I was discussing with a friend how a dance floor, even a punk show mosh pit, should be a place of community. Brownian motion where the crowd moves and bounces synergistically with each other. If someone falls, stop and make sure the person is ok. How do you respond to potentially violent and/or inappropriate conduct in that setting? Do you respond in kind, or "when they go low, we go high."

It is not a new argument/quandary, and it is worth considering, debating in a group less than 10 even, whether "[r]eturning violence for violence multiplies violence," or whether we need to establish equality "by any means necessary."

As for me, I will continue to apply a measured approach to protect myself and others through words and deeds. To the extent I can--

though it gets harder with age--, I inevitably hang on the edge of the mosh pit, uniting with like-minded individuals, hopefully larger and stronger than I am, to serve as an ad hoc buffer to allow the moshers to have their fun, watch out for people or things that are falling/flying and let the others enjoy watching the performance. But, serving in that shield capacity, once in a while a push and/or strong words are necessary to maintain the line in my supposed attempt to achieve a greater good for the temporary society.

I am not sure I am acting or choosing not to act in the right way. Maybe in responding I am contributing to more darkness than light. Does my physical reaction beget more violence? Maybe when I don't act I am permitting harm or potential harm to others that I would have prevented through action. Maybe Kathleen Hanna would be willing to talk with me or co-write an article about that this weekend.

Though confusion may be my epitaph, I have a lot of clarity about where I will be Saturday night. Sportsman's Club, 948 North Western (Augusta and Western). From 10 pm to close in a totally unofficial Riotfest afterparty mode, thoughtfully playing vinyl including Riotfest acts.

If you're a rock star, porn star, super star, doesn't matter what you are -get off your ar___ over there.

Chapter 36: I Want To Believe-SPORTSMAN'S CLUB SATURDAY 10/12 - AND-- MUSEUM OF CONTEMPORARY ART FRIDAY 10/19

Subject: I Want To Believe-SPORTSMAN'S CLUB SATURDAY 10/12 - AND-- MUSEUM OF CONTEMPORARY ART FRIDAY 10/19

From: Lazar, Bart
Sent: Thu, Oct 10, 2019, 11:28 PM

When asked if he believes in astrology, Nick Cave responded "He Believes in the Right to Believe" and proceeded that though he is unsure whether G-d exists, he chooses to live his life in a manner as if there is a G-d.

Does a belief system require belief, or is the challenging and questioning of the belief structure, somehow its own creation of a critical framework of its own.

I can feel something inside me say, belief is one ability we all can share, we can choose to share that ability towards different approaches.

A feminist Rabbinical student approached a major theme of the Jewish New Year- that G-d reigns as King among Kings from a throne up high. As Americans, she noted, we don't really believe in Kings to whom we submit our sovereignty, and moreover, inclusive egalitarian people do not ascribe to the belief of a masculine ruler. Yet, we can all, as individuals, close our eyes together and attempt to visualize what we believe a ruler or ruling force likes like, the place that the ruler inhabits, and maybe observe the ruler as it goes about whatever it does or does not do.

Even in our version of a reality, a ruler can be beyond belief.

But different beliefs can share common paths and goals and lead to understanding.

We believe in the weather. We believe in changes in the weather.

We hope for a change in the weather, a change for the better can brighten up our day.

I really do think we're strong enough.

I believe that I (and you) have two great places to interact and share our beliefs-- This Saturday---October 12, the monthly, usual, but always new and different Sportsman's Club DJ thing. But also a week from Friday, I will be DJ-ing at the Museum of Contemporary Art celebrating the Chicago premiere of the lauded American teen noir film Knives & Skin, showing as part of the Chicago International Film Festival--which connects me with Boy George in two ways--he DJ'd at the MCA too, and his song is featured In the movie. The movie is great so check out us both.

Sportsman's Club --Saturday, October 12, 10pm to close Museum of Contemporary Art Friday October 18 -9-11 movie, 11-1230 or so party.
948 N. Western Avenue 220 E. Chicago Avenue

I BELIEVE (Pete Shelley)

Declaration of (Dis) Interest

In these times of contention, it's not my intention to make things plain
I'm looking through mirrors to catch the reflection that can't be mine
I'm losing control now, I'll just have to slow down a thought or two
I can't feel the future and I'm not even certain that there is a past

I believe in the worker's revolution
And I believe in the final solution
I believe in, I believe in
I believe in the shape of things to come
And I believe, I'm not the only one
Yes, I believe in, I believe in

When I poison my system, I take thoughts and twist them into shapes
I'm reachin' my nadir and I haven't an idea of what to do
I'm painting by numbers but can't find the colors that fill you in
I'm not even knowing if I'm coming or going, if to end or begin

I believe in the immaculate conception
And I believe in the resurrection
And I believe in, I believe in
I believe in the elixir of youth
And I believe in the absolute truth
Yes I believe in, I believe in

There is no love in this world anymore
There is no love in this world anymore

I've fallen from favor while tryin' to savor experience
I'm seein' things clearly but it has quite nearly blown my mind
It's the aim of existence to offer resistance to the flow of time
Everything is and that is why, it is will be the line

I believe in perpetual motion
And I believe in perfect devotion
I believe in, I believe in

I believe in the things I've never had
And I believe in my mum and my dad
And I believe in, I believe in

There is no love in this world anymore
There is no love in this world anymore

I'm skippin' the pages of a book that takes ages for the foreword to end
Triangular cover concealing another aspect from view
My relative motion is just an illusion from stopping too fast
The essence of being these feelings I'm feeling, I just want them to last

I believe in original sin
And I believe what I believe in
Yes I believe in, I believe in
I believe in the web of fate
And I believe, I'm goin' to be late
So I'll be leavin', what I believe in

There is no love in this world anymore
There is no love in this world anymore
There is no love in this world anymore
There is no love in this world anymore
There is no love in this world anymore
There is no love in this world anymore
There is no love in this world anymore
There is no love in this world anymore
There is no love in this world anymore
There is no love in this world anymore

Chapter 37: Rising Above 2019 (and an exclusive)--Sportsmans Club Saturday December 14

Subject: Rising Above 2019 (and an exclusive)--Sportsmans Club Saturday December 14

From: Lazar, Bart
Sent: Thu, Dec 12, 2019, 3:37 PM

Maybe I immersed myself more in music this year to avoid aspects of the world that shall not be named. Whatever the reason, I experiences so many great performances both from new, old and even in between artists this year (even The Rolling Stones were tremendous).

Don't bemoan the lack of quality new music, at least I can vouch for qualified candidates! We all have the chance. Ignore reality--just for one day or a couple of hours--that and Matzo ball soup will heal you.

You can ignore or embrace reality with me and assist in healing, venting, celebrating out at Sportsman's Club to finish out 2019 this Saturday. In addition to the 50 + years of vinyl I will be debuting the Nick Zinner's (Yeah Yeah Yeahs) soundtrack for the movie Knives and Skin. The movie is opening Friday at the Music Box theatre for a week's run and is worth your time. Here is Richard Roeper's review:

https://chicago.suntimes.com/2019/12/5/20993035/knives-skin-review-movie-film-jennifer-reeder-chicago.

SPORTSMANS CLUB-- 948 N. Western. Saturday December 14 from 10-2:45

Here are some nuggets of some of the best performances I witnessed in 2019.

Best Performances by "Newer" Performers

Fontaines DC (Lincoln Hall, Latitude 30) - You'd think that this post-punk band from Dublin hales from Manchester because of its lead singer's pent up Ian Curtis aggressive and energetic pacing and blurting Mark E. Smith speak/sing. Powerful. Boys in the Better Land has a People Who Died flare.

The Beths (Cheer Up Charlies, Scoot Inn, Logan Square Arts Festival). New Zealand's top power pop band delivers jangly riffs and creative lyrics. The Future Me Hates Me may be the best song of 2019.

Pip Blom (Lazarus Brewing) A surprise treat from the Netherlands, features a sister (Pip)/brother (Tender) band combo dishing out snarling vocals over grungy guitars. Check out Daddy Issues.

Pottymouth (Sleeping Village, B.D. Riley's) LA's pop punk quartet conquers its audience with brash, sharp, infectious power chords and high energy dance.

Chai (Pitchfork, Mohawk) Sometimes performance can transcend musical and geographical borders. You have to love these 4 young women (including identical twins) from Nagoya Japan whose walk on music is a rip off of CSS. They are so infectiously cute (Kawaii in Japanese), that their synchronized dancing and synth dance music makes everyone have their own cute smile. See them January 25 at the Empty Bottle.

Ratboys (Square Roots, Cheer Up Charlies). Americana-ish almost country indie rock from the foreign country of Chicago! Upbeat, jangly and rootsy.

Viagra Boys (Empty Bottle, Swan Dive) This Swedish band has the worst name, but sounds the most like Iggy and the Stooges, with a thick, buzzing, guttural grinding combination of punky guitars and sax, and a shirtless, bloated, overly tattooed front man who clearly does not give.

Ezra Collective (Latitude 30) Straight ahead upbeat urban urbane jazz standard bearers from London.

Negative Scanner (Frozen Dancing, Bric a Brac) Newish by now, this Chicago DIY-punk quartet provides more power in 30 minutes than most bands can muster in a year.

Best Performances by "Older" Performers

Bikini Kill (Riotfest). Kathleen Hanna is one of the most dynamic performers alive and it was a treat to mosh with women and men of all ages to her original Riotgrrl bullets against our exclusionary society. Everyone to the front

Wreckless Eric (Burlington). In the delivery vs. expectation department Eric probably won for the year. He is unabashedly a one hit wonder from 42 years ago (Whole Wide World) that bears his soul with electrified folk songs and social commentary.

Mekons (Hideout, Square Roots, High Noon Saloon) Through thin and thick these cow punks return from all parts of the globe to record an album and perform and do at tour. Their layered sounds and political bent are so on point.

<u>Television (Old Town School, Phoenix Concert Theatre)</u> The intricate and interweaving guitar work of Tom Verlaine and his long time collaborators remains magical 40+ years on.

<u>B 52s (Riotfest)</u> If you want to dance--Dance!

<u>Flesheaters (Lincoln Hall)</u> The LA punk rock supergroup you might never have heard of relaunched featuring X' John Doe and DJ Bonebrake, Dave Alvin (Blasters) and leader/poet Chris dirty, grinding blues-abilly.

<u>King Crimson (Auditorium)</u> Robert Fripp went full percussion throttle with three drummers mashing drum line with proto-metal rock.

<u>Omara Portunado (Old Town School)</u> At 89 years old, the grand dame of the Buena Vista Social Club gave her last tour with rhythm, soul, charisma, romance and love.

<u>Nick Cave (Copernicus Center)</u> In answering audience questions and solo performance, the lounge lizard from hell taught us how to channel and handle grief with elegy and furor.

<u>Dave Davies (City Winery/Space)</u> He's not like everybody else, including his brother Ray.

<u>Billy Bragg (Lincoln Hall)</u> Even with a raspy throat, this old punk can sing and tell us more about American politics and ourselves than most anyone else.

Cinghiale (Elastic Arts) Reedists Ken Vandermark and Mars Williams energetically emit honks and snorts with visceral impact.

Rise Above--Greg Ginn
Jealous cowards try to control
Rise above! We're gonna rise above!

They distort what we say
Rise above! We're gonna rise above!
Try and stop what we do
Rise above! We're gonna rise above!
When they can't do it themselves
Rise above! We're gonna rise above!
We are tired of your abuse
Try to stop us, it's no use
Society's arms of control
Rise above! We're gonna rise above!
Think they're smart, can't think for themselves
Rise above! We're gonna rise above!
Laugh at us behind our backs
Rise above! We're gonna rise above!
I find satisfaction in what they lack
Rise above! We're gonna rise above!
We are tired of your abuse
Try to stop us, it's no use
We are tired of your abuse
Try to stop us, it's no use
We're born with a chance
Rise above! We're gonna rise above!
I am gonna have my chance
Rise above! We're gonna rise above!
We're born with a chance
Rise above! We're gonna rise above!
And I am gonna have my chance
Rise above! We're gonna rise above!
We are tired of your abuse
Try to stop us it's no use
Rise above! Rise above!
Rise above! We're gonna rise above!
We're gonna rise above! We're gonna rise above!

Chapter 38: Savor Positive Memories In the New Year--DJ Thing Continues for its Sixth Year

Subject: Savor Positive Memories In the New Year--DJ Thing Continues for its Sixth Year

From: Lazar, Bart
Sent: Fri, Jan 10, 5:55 PM

Our life is looking forward or its looking back. That's it. That's our life. Where's the Moment? -Ricky Roma.

Are our new experiences silver or gold. Are our memories golden or irrelevant. Does taking that phone photo detract from the moment or improve future memory? Does the artificial line between last year and this year real or virtual? And, if it is really artificial why all the questions?

Time is a funny thing, and a peculiar item. Nostalgia may be the gateway drug to disconnection from the present and the future, while archeology may connect them.

Forward looking statement: I am excited by starting my sixth year at Sportman's, looking in the rear view mirror for the strict purpose of merging the old with the new, vinyl music wise. Whether that assists you in looking backward by reliving a moment, look forward by building on your knowledge, you can just hang with friends and/or an awesome cocktail while a pre and post punk progressive pop soundtrack plays in the background---

Hey Ricky/David, all of you---THERE is the moment. SPORTSMANS CLUB-- 948 N. Western. Saturday January 10, 2020 from 10-2:45

Chapter 39: Being Good -Andy Gill, Society and Me -Sportsman's Club and You ---Saturday February 8.

Subject: Being Good -Andy Gill, Society and Me - Sportsman's Club and You ---Saturday February 8.

From: Lazar, Bart
Sent: Fri, Feb 7, 2020, 3:15 PM

There is so much in flux in the world today -- truth, faith, science - - . Can it all be doubted or weaponized for self-interest?

Sadly, we know the answer is yes, and as a result we are fractured in too many pieces.

We may live as we dream, alone --but what separates the two, and what separates our individuality and collectiveness is something that we each can choose.

Words and actions matter, and it is not just work that defines ourselves, even if sometimes in the minds of others it is.

I had the privilege of perceiving the work product of Andy Gill for 40 some-odd years. My memory enhanced by technology tells me I first saw him perform at Hurrah in NY in 1981 and Instagram tells me I last saw him perform at Space in Evanston last February. His fierce, measured, unsettling guitar bursts and stoic nature both defined and contrasted with the danceable Post Punk sound and disturbing political vision. He was great at what he did.

Words fail me now, except that good is an innate quality. Good is better than ok and looks out for the interests of others. Good may be doubted in the short term but can be weaponized in a non-violent way. Despite our own individual questions regarding whether and what one person can do--fatalism is not the answer, we did not start that way.

Feel free to exercise your individual right to choose by fitting a visit to Sportsman's Club tomorrow into your schedule. There will certainly be a dose of the Gang of Four together with other pre- and post-punk progressive pop and indie offerings. And find an Andy Gill/Gang of Four performance on YouTube.

Sportsman's Club, 948 N. Western Avenue
Saturday February 8, from 10 pm to close.

Blinkered, paralysed
Flat on my back

They say our world is built on endeavor
That every man is for himself
Wealth is for the one that wants it
Paradise, if you can earn it

History is the reason
I'm washed up

Blinkered, paralysed
Flat on my back

My ambitions come to nothing
What I wanted now just seems a waste of time
I can't make out what has gone wrong

I was good at what I did

The crows come home to roost
And I'm the dupe

© Andy Gill/Jon King

And, by the way, my blog www.oldpunksrule.com is back and active. New posts coming soon (probably after SXSW).

Chapter 40: Be Safe, Well, Sane (up to a point) and Yes, Please Thrive. Fake Sportsman's DJ Thing, Whatever Day it Might Be

Subject: Be Safe, Well, Sane (up to a point) and Yes, Please Thrive. Fake Sportsman's DJ Thing, Whatever Day it Might Be

From: Lazar, Bart
Sent: Sat, May 16, 2020, 1:21 PM

Be Safe, Well, Sane (up to a point) and Yes, Please Thrive. Fake Sportsman's DJ Thing, Whatever Day it Might Be

In the lead track from Diet Cig's great new album Do You Wonder About Me?, Alex Luciano wants to know whether someone who mistreated her is thinking about her. She wants to know mostly because "I just want you to know that I'm thriving. Thanks for asking."

While it is not human, in our two month relationship with the pandemic it certainly asks us questions about how we are every day. And while it is most important that you and yours are all safe, well and reasonably sane- is there anything wrong with thriving?

In the midst of an unknown force (yes, sometimes combined with the usual known evil empire) trying to bring us down, positivity is all around. There are people helping strangers, neighbors, friends and family with acts of kindness great and subtle. Businesses have adapted to help others as well as themselves. We have learned new skills, to make masks, teach and learn how to cook new foods and make new drinks, create new spaces and make new uses out of old/existing ones, video experience, strengthen personal relationships in profound if unexpected ways, and perhaps most importantly, build comfort and confidence in the knowledge of our personal resilience--all simultaneously wishing every moment it will just end already.

So, yeah, in my caring but pc way I wish you and yours are all safe, well and somewhat sane, but to tell you what I really, really want is for all of us to give cv the proverbial middle finger, put our fists in the air or bang your pots and pans (spit in the face, however, is no longer appropriate rebellious idiom, sorry Bruce) and collectively say "I'm thriving thanks for asking."

This is the third Sportsmans set I am missing, and I have been creating simulacra playlists on Spotify. I'll be putting up a new one tonight or tomorrow [after all time is really relative right now] at @blazar331 on Spotify where you can also check out some of my restaurant soundtracks, including a folksy one and even a radio show playlist from 1983. See you soon, but in the meantime say safe, healthy, reasonably sane, strong, confident, surviving and yes thriving.

Virtual Sportsman's Club dj thing simulacrum.
Blazar331

Today, tomorrow or whatever day it might be, it could be or it is.

About the Author

©2015 Mitchell A. Lazar

Bart Lazar started as a radio disc jockey in 1977 and was part of the first wave of punk, post punk and new wave dj's in Chicago. Today he is a punk and roll vinyl only dj exploring common sounds and ground between genres and generations. He plays old music that sounds new, new music that sounds old and great music that sounds great. One set will cover 50 years of rock n roll, from the British Invasion, garage music of the 60s, pre and post punk progressive pop of the 70s and 80s and the indie/psych/garage scenes of today. You'll hear unique cover songs, spaghetti westerns and some surprises too. Bart has performed at venues such as Taste of Chicago, Museum of Contemporary Art, Delilah's, Club Foot and The Crocodile and has had a multi-year residency at Sportsman's Club in Chicago. He is also is a music journalist, writing for www.newcity.com and his blog www.oldpunksrule.com.

Gallery

2018 Aug 17 Middlebrow

© 2017 Bart A. Lazar -- Dec 29 2017

Dec 29 2018

Jan 27 2017

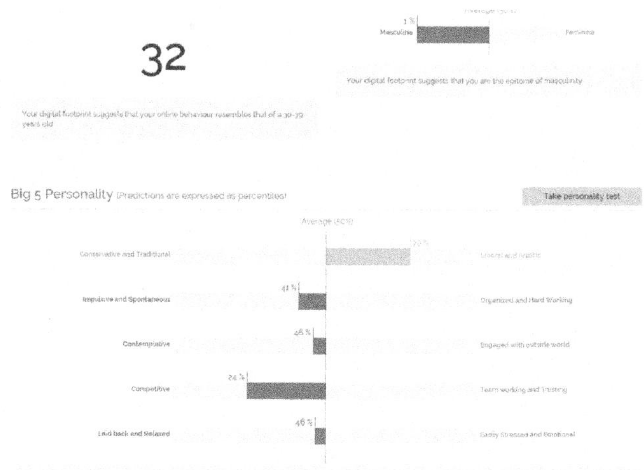

March 22 2018

May 26 2016

May 26 2016

Movie Premiere

SECRET DRUM BAND

2018 National Tour

Performance by Secret Drum Band with special lecture, "Documenting Ecosystems" presented by Lisa Schonberg

Thursday, March 29 | 5:00pm

International House

1414 E. 59th St, Chicago, IL 60637

Free and open to the public

Event Schedule

5:00pm | Doors open, reception and exhibitions begin
6:00pm | Lecture and multimedia presentation
6:45pm | Q&A
7:00pm | Intermission
7:30pm | Performance

Presented by the **Global Voices Performing Arts Series** and made possible in part by the generous support from Bart Lazar, AB'82.
Additional cosponsors include:

ARTS
SCIENCE +
CULTURE
INITIATIVE

FRIZZELL
SPEAKER &
LEARNING
SERIES

Persons with disabilities who may require assistance should contact the Office of Programs and External Relations in advance of the program at 773.753.2274 or mdestefa@uchicago.edu

Dec 29 2018 Secret Drum Band

Made in the USA
Monee, IL
21 December 2021